THE ANTIDOTE TO FEAR

Overcoming Hardships to Build a Successful Business and a Fulfilling Life

BY KRIS MURRAY

Edited by Lil Barcaski

Published by: GWN Publishing
www.GWNPublishing.com

Cover Design: Kristina Conatser

ISBN: 978-1-965971-22-2

DEDICATION

I dedicate this book to heart-centered, passionate entrepreneurs everywhere.

TABLE OF CONTENTS

ENDORSEMENTS

"Kris Murray has written a book that is as courageous as it is practical. The Antidote to Fear is honest, relatable, and grounded in real-life experience. She shows how fear, when faced directly, can become a catalyst for growth, and she provides strategies that are both clear and actionable. For anyone navigating uncertainty in life or business, this book offers steady guidance and encouragement."

DR. MARSHALL GOLDSMITH
Thinkers50 #1 Executive Coach and New York Times
bestselling author of *The Earned Life, Triggers,*
and *What Got You Here Won't Get You There*
www.marshallgoldsmith.com

"Kris is someone who is never afraid to tackle the hard things and follow bold visions and then comes out the other side with learnings and deep empathy (along with an infectious wit and smile) for others on the path. Whether it's for entrepreneurs she mentors or simply someone that can be there for anything going on in your life. She is someone you want in your corner."

YANIK SILVER
author *Evolved Enterprise,* and founder Maverick1000
https://maverick1000.com/

"I've known Kris Murray for years, and was thrilled when she joined us in The Trust. She is a SUPER-smart business strategist. And she's a blast to hang with. Kris's new book The Antidote to Fear is a **must-read**... packed with personal and business stories that will change how you look at your work and your life forever."

ALI BROWN
Founder of The Trust and star of ABC's *Secret Millionaire*
www.jointhetrust.org

"If you're looking for change, you need to find a coach that's been through it all, and who has gone to great depths to come out the other side. Kris Murray is that person. She's got the experience and a modern aged wisdom that can create that change you've been looking for. Her new book The Antidote to Fear is a great place to start."

AMIR ZOGHI,
Mindset Coach | Transformation Facilitator
| International Speaker
www.Amirzoghi.com

"Kris Murray has been a pivotal influence in our journey, and we found her at the perfect time. The growth we experienced was significantly fueled by our time learning from her. She continues to inspire with her unique blend of courage, wisdom, and clarity. The Antidote to Fear reflects that same energy! It is insightful, bold, and deeply encouraging."

JULIE ROY
Entrepreneur, Investor, and Founder of WealthMasters
www.Thejulieroy.com

"Kris Murray has transformed the lives of thousands of leaders and entrepreneurs. With The Antidote to Fear, she shares her blueprint for how to create wealth, freedom, and love in your life, based on her own experiences. If you're looking for a mentor who knows her stuff, you've found an extraordinary one in Kris."

ANDRE NORMAN
Founder of Second Chance University
www.secondchanceuniversity.org

"The Antidote to Fear is the perfect choice to help you get unstuck! Whether you have a dream that is waiting on the sidelines out of fear, or you've just made the biggest move of your life and you're wondering. 'Can I really do this?' consider this your guide through.

"Written in fun and easy to digest stories, Kris Murray gets to the heart of the matter about what it takes to move through fear. And fear really is under every one of our less than ideal results in life! Personal transformation requires we move through fear. So pick a chapter and get moving."

DARLA LEDOUX
Author of *Shift the Field* and *Retreat and Grow Rich*

'Having known Kris Murray as a dedicated coach and supportive friend, I can attest to the profound impact of her insights, which shine through in The Antidote to Fear. *This book feels like a heartfelt conversation, offering comfort and actionable steps to embrace life's uncertainties. Kris's memoir is an invaluable resource for aspiring business leaders and anyone looking to build a life of purpose."*

TAMEENAH ADAMS
Serial Entrepreneur and Director of Coaching,
The Child Care Success Company
www.childcaresuccess.com

"When I met Kris Murray, I was scaling fast and feeling both excited and overwhelmed. She didn't just give me strategies—she gave me courage and the push to trust myself as a leader. Kris has a gift for saying the hard things with boldness and encouragement and The Antidote to Fear carries that same power: honest, practical, and filled with truth that moves leaders forward with grit and grace."

RACHEL SUPALLA
8-Figure Founder | CEO | Best-Selling Author | Business
Consultant | TED Speaker | Playful Leadership Advocate

"Wow! Kris Murray presents a wonderful resource for everyone who is looking for real assistance addressing the fears that on occasion can hold a grip on any of us, personally and professionally. The Antidote of Fear uses real-life examples which Kris herself experienced and overcame using her described ten antidotes."

ANN RHOADES
President and Founder, PeopleInk
Co-Founder, JetBlue Airways

"Kris Murray has a gift for opening doors to possibilities most of us never imagined. In "The Antidote to Fear," she shares with honesty and courage—the wins, the struggles, and the lessons—that have been life-changing for me both in business and in life. This book carries that same authenticity and wisdom, offering readers the clarity and confidence to reshape their business and their future."

VERNON MASON, JR., M.ED.
Best-Selling Author, Humorist, Inspiring Keynote Speaker
www.vernonmason.com

PREFACE

The alarm went off next to my bed. My eyes flashed open. An immediate ball of dread landed in my stomach like a shot. I lay there, looking at the ceiling, thinking about the day ahead. I thought to myself, "What if I pull the covers over my head and hide from the world? Can my kids and my business keep going without me, just for one day?"

My life was in the shitter, and I didn't think I could face it. Two weeks prior, a trusted employee of mine, who I depended on and believed in with all my heart, sued me out of the blue for $850,000. My 14-year-old son was in trouble with the local police and got suspended from school. And to top it all off, I went out on St. Patty's Day to drown my sorrows and got a DUI. I had to spend a night in jail and sobbed with heartbreak all night behind bars. I had hit my rock bottom. I felt humiliated, ashamed, and scared.

I was flat on the mat. I had no more "positive mindset" to give and no one to help me through this mess. Hell, I didn't even have a driver's license. Because of the DUI, my license was revoked for 90 days, even though it was the first time in my life I had ever been in any trouble. Every day I risked more jail time to drive my kids illegally to school. You see, there was no Uber or other options in my tiny town of Crested Butte, Colorado. And I was a full-time single mom of two teens.

In my business, things were close to collapsing. When my former employee left, I had to immediately hire a high-powered (read – expensive) attorney firm in Denver to fight the lawsuit. Then I had to take back the entire large client load that she had been covering, doubling the number of hours spent on one-on-one coaching calls. I was cash- and time-strapped and had no earthly clue how much longer I could hold on. The day-to-day stress was almost unbearable.

That morning in early April 2017, I wanted to give up. I was afraid to put my feet on the floor and face the day. The fear inside of me was deeply paralyzing. How was I going to find the courage to right the ship, save my family, and save my business?

INTRODUCTION

I meet so many people who are stopped by fear. Fear of what others think, fear of discomfort, fear of the unknown. Fear that an imagined crisis or tragedy might happen.

Fear keeps people small. More than anything else, fear can keep you stuck in an unhappy life or send you down a path that's unfulfilling, ill-suited to you, or downright disastrous.

As a business coach, I have helped thousands of people face their fears. I have watched them take baby steps, small actions to conquer the fear. To lay it down. To release it and let go. My hope is that this book, while allowing me to tell my story, will touch the heart of you, the reader, in a fresh way to help you release fear.

One of the first sayings that I became known for as a coach and speaker was, "Action is the antidote to fear." That sounds really simple, right? Just take action in the face of fear. But sometimes, even the tiniest baby step can feel impossible to take, if fear has you in its grasp.

A similar quote you've probably heard is "do it afraid." One of my mentors is Dan Sullivan, founder of Strategic Coach. Dan is famous for saying "Do it with wet pants." In other words, if you feel like you're so afraid you're going to pee your pants, go ahead, then do it with wet pants anyway. I love this metaphor and have shared it often.

I have a confession to make. Even though I coach others to "just take action" to conquer fear, I have sat with various outlines and starter versions of this book for over a year—doing nothing to move it forward, let alone get it done. Feeling stuck. Procrastinating. I even caused myself to get a case of nervous hives thinking about trying to get going again! The lessons I am learning about fear WHILE WRITING these very words have been transformative.

So, even though I have conquered many fears and created an 8-figure empire from scratch, I can still go through deep processes around fear in my life. My guess is that even mega-billionaires like Bezos and Buffett still get caught up by fear. It never leaves you. The good news is, it's a practice. I have a practice where I can laugh at these fears, process them, and let them go in order to move forward. As you grow in your capacity as a human, an entrepreneur, a parent, just about anything—**your capacity to process fear gets stronger**. I want to help you process your fears and let them go. I will be sharing many ways of doing this throughout this book.

There are many antidotes to fear. One is based on the age-old acronym "False Experiences Appearing Real." Tapping back into your inner knowing, or intuition, will show you that your fear is usually imagined. It's a false belief in your mind that you see as REAL. The "antidote" is to realize that you're being victimized by your fear-based mindset and to shift that mindset. Throughout this book, as I tell my story of business and personal challenges and how I overcame them, I will share the strategies I used to conquer the fears. To USE that fear energy and *power it into wins.*

Speaking of wins, this is another strategy for conquering fear. Notice and celebrate your wins. This is how we always start coaching calls with clients in the company I founded—the Child Care Success Company. This is how we begin: what's a recent WIN you are proud of? What's new and good? Wins build confidence, and confidence is an important lever in your toolkit for overcoming fear. I'll share more about how I used this strategy to conquer fear, and how you can too, in Chapter Seven.

Like many of you, I have faced my share of sleepless nights. Even when you feel like you can't move forward and you don't have the will to get out of bed to face your fears, I hope this book can be a catalyst to get you moving through it. (Trust me, I was there).

Throughout this book as I share the story of creating businesses and facing fears on the journey, three themes emerge: *abundance, freedom, and love*. These are also the core values for how I live my life and how I coach others. Abundance, for an abundant mindset which creates a wealthy life. And here I mean wealth not just in terms of money—it's having a wealth of joy and beautiful experiences. Abundance, or wealth, fuels the freedom you have in your choices and **your ability to accomplish whatever you desire**. And a freedom mindset keeps your heart open to whatever shows up. Finally, at the end of the day, it's about love. Love for yourself is first and foremost. After that, it's about creating love in your life in all different aspects—with God (or Source), with family and friends, with the clients you serve and the teammates you work with.

I invite you to be aware of how these three themes show up for you as you read the book, and hopefully, complete the exercises at the end of each chapter. It's my ultimate wish to help you have more abundance, freedom, and love in your life.

BUSINESS IS IN MY BLOOD – HOW I GREW UP

Being around small "Main Street" businesses was part of my childhood and part of my DNA. I never really realized how much entrepreneurship was a natural part of my life until I was a guest on Chaz Wolfe's *Gather the Kings* podcast just a couple years ago. Chaz asked me what formed my reality as a kid, regarding the seeds of entrepreneurship. I started telling him the story of all the businesses that my grandparents and parents built, and all of a sudden, it hit me like a ton of bricks! I was the pure product of business owners, on both sides of my family and for several generations before me. Until that moment, I never consciously realized how much my childhood was influenced by business and entrepreneurship.

KOCIAN MEATS

My grandparents on my dad's side owned Kocian Meats, a thriving and very popular meat market and butcher shop in downtown Cleveland, Ohio, where I was born. (Kocian is my maiden name). The business still exists today, run by my cousins. Some of the first memories of my childhood were there.

My dad and his three brothers were expected to show up every Saturday and work the market and help out my grandparents on their busiest day of the week. The place was jammed with customers, all taking numbers and buying their week's worth of ribs, steaks, and other various products. It could get pretty wild, and the energy was electric. The only forms of payment back then were cash or food stamps. My grandparents would mostly hang out in their back office and manage the place, do the finances, and buy meat wholesale.

When I got old enough—about eight or nine years-old—I was put to work too. My job was to count money. I was really good at counting. I almost never made a mistake, and I felt very proud of my accuracy. I was taught to count, double count, and even triple count the money and put it in piles, then wrap it in groups of hundreds or thousands. At the end of a workday, I was given some cash for a job well done—usually 10 or 20 bucks, which was a lot back then for a kid.

This instilled a strong work ethic in me, and I liked to make my grandparents proud. I also got to observe them managing and leading their employees. I was a "fly on the wall" for their work and personal conversations. Employees would knock on the office door and ask for special favors from my grandfather. He was a little like the Godfather in those moments—come kiss the ring and get a little extra. This made a big impression on me, but it was kind of unconscious/subconscious. I saw the power of owning a successful business. I saw what it was like to have wealth and be the owner of something that others envied.

One thing I still remember is a framed plaque they had on the wall in the office. It said:

> *"Low class people talk about other people.*
> *Middle class people talk about possessions.*
> *Wealthy people talk about ideas and dreams."*

That sign made a big impression on me. I wanted to become someone who talks about ideas and dreams. The seed was planted.

CHAPMAN JEWELERS

My mother's parents also had a business, but it was VERY different than an urban meat business. They lived about two hours west of us in the farmland of northwest Ohio. Gram and Gramp had a large farm as well as a thriving jewelry store business—Chapman Jewelers—in a small town called Fostoria. That's where my mom grew up. My grandpa bought the farm as a semi-retirement step because he also raised Morgan horses and took them to shows. We got to go with them a couple times to the horse shows. They sold Chapman Jewelers when I was about nine years old, and just did the horse farm thing. My brother and I LOVED to spend summers at the farm, running through the corn fields, riding horses, and trying to catch the wild kittens in the barn.

Being on the farm gave me a taste of a whole different kind of freedom. Plus, farm life was an interesting juxtaposition to the urban city environment of Kocian Meats. Before they sold the jewelry store, we'd go visit them there sometimes during the workday. My grandma was always doing one of two things at her store: selling, or building relationships with potential customers for a future sale. She was a natural born salesperson, someone who "never met a stranger." She could make friends with anyone, even someone she secretly did not like.

My grandfather was the watch expert. He could fix pretty much any watch. He was always in the back office doing jewelry repairs or other behind the scenes work. He was the quiet one of the pair, happy to not have to deal with the front of the store. Again, looking back, I can see how this impacted me by showing me pride in ownership. Now I had two examples of business success—one in the urban city center and one in the rural countryside.

MY MOM: A MAIN STREET BUSINESS OWNER

My mom, Barbara, was an only child and felt pretty stifled by her parents growing up. Of course, she grew up with the examples of her parents owning the successful jewelry business, where she also helped out, so she became an expert at retail. My mom has great taste, and I mean *great*! She has an eye for making things look good, whether it's fashion, merchandising, or home design. It made perfect sense that she and my stepdad would start a retail business on Main Street USA. They bought an office supply and bookstore in downtown Sarasota, Florida, in 1980, and moved my brother and I down there to have a new life after my parents divorced and she remarried.

So, instead of going to high school in the Cleveland area, I became a beach town kid, hanging out on Siesta Key beach. In Southwest Florida, the families were more transient, and the education was not as high quality as Ohio schools, but we made it work. My first real job, other than counting cash at the meat market, was working in the office supply store. By then, I was 13 years old. I found restocking the shelves and changing window displays quite boring, but I liked serving customers.

I loved helping people find what they were looking for and putting a smile on their faces. Then I got to move over to the bookstore side, and later to the Campus Book Store serving the University of South Florida. That was a really fun job because our customers were mostly college students and professors. One time, right after the Presidential election, a student came in and said, "I'm looking for a Greek Tragedy." Instantly I retorted, "Sorry, but Michael Dukakis isn't here at the moment." Everyone in the store cracked up and I realized I could sometimes have a quick wit.

MY DAD: A HUGE INFLUENCE

My dad was one of six kids who grew up in a very competitive household. It seemed like all the siblings had rivalries with one another, and especially my dad with his three brothers. They were all trying to gain the favor of my grandfather. My dad was extremely driven to be successful, especially in his thirties. He and my mom married very young, and both my brother and I were born by the time my dad was 24. He was a CPA, had a side business in Hartford, and various other "deals" that he always seemed to be working. He made some good moves but also lost a bunch of money. He was a real mover and shaker, sometimes to the detriment of his personal relationships. He and my mom divorced when I was seven.

Dad would often take my brother and I with him on his various business "errands." So again, I was the fly on the wall for his dealmaking. It seemed like he was always on the verge of creating that eight-figure business he dreamed of, but it never quite worked out. Yet, we had some great conversations about business during our car rides. One I will never forget is when I was about 14 years old and Dad asked me, "What's the purpose of any business?" I think my answer was something like, "making money" or "being profitable." He said, "Close. But no. I believe it's to get and keep customers." So, he was always thinking about how to deliver value to customers and clients. This instilled a great truth in me—which is to focus on VALUE.

My dad was an early business coach, before coaching was "a thing". He was also a very talented speaker and leader. To this day, I still have some of his journals from attending leadership and communication seminars when he was in his forties. In those, he wrote extensively about wanting to start a business coaching practice teach seminars on success principles. Later in this book, as I describe how I created a 7-figure coaching business and ran big successful conferences, it's evident how much I followed in my dad's footsteps. I brought to fruition a dream that he had for himself but never accomplished.

My dad died suddenly at 63 years old of a heart attack. He was found on the side of the road from a passer-by when he was on a walk in the neighborhood. He died instantly. I felt so heartbroken when my dad died. Like I had lost my lifeline. The first night after it happened, I could not sleep. I remember pretending that he was still alive, and I made up a story in my mind that I'd see him tomorrow just so I could fall asleep in my pretend world.

At this point, I was married with an infant and a three-year-old. About a year after my dad died, I seriously began thinking about starting my own business. Maybe his death made me stop "waiting" for the right time to jump in—because life is fleeting and I needed to start my dreams sooner rather than later.

When I started my business, I had $15,000 in seed money from my dad's passing. Other than that, I put everything on credit cards to start and grow the business. As of the writing of this book, I took that $15,000 in seed money and built two businesses with a combined value of over $12 million dollars. I share this not to wow or impress you, but to demonstrate that there can be a huge payoff when you flex the muscle of working through your fears. **The money is just a reflection of playing a bigger game, and the value that was created as a result**. Whether you want to make more money, build highly successful companies, or just live a life of more freedom and happiness, this book can help you on your path.

One more thing—while I speak about my journey building a business in the early childhood/daycare field, the specific *type* of business is irrelevant. The business success I created and the principles I share in this book can apply to ANY type of business, in any niche.

Ready to dig in? Let's go.

"Our job in this lifetime is not to shape ourselves into some ideal we imagine we ought to be, but to find out who we already are and become it."

– STEVEN PRESSFIELD, THE WAR OF ART

CHAPTER ONE

FOLLOW YOUR FEELING

Thursday was my favorite day. That was the day I got to be home with my kids and just be together. Our typical Thursday routine was to go to "Mommy yoga class" and then to McDonald's for lunch. The best part of that particular McDonald's was a massive PlayPlace where the kids would climb and play for hours with the other kids. I usually got a salad and, of course, the kids got Happy Meals.

We had this really cool set-up where one of our town's best yoga teachers would come to the home of a local mom and we'd practice yoga in her basement rec room. First, we would drop all of our kids off at the house across the street where there were two nannies waiting to welcome them. It was 90 minutes of bliss and connection for about eight moms in the neighborhood every week. And the kids had a blast at their weekly playdate, too.

One day in the spring of 2007, I was almost done with class and in the final pose of complete relaxation, known as Shivasana or corpse pose. In other words, I was in utter stillness. No mind, just breath. As clear as the clearest thought you can imagine, it came in. The voice or the inner knowing said quite clearly "childcare." I recall being in a state of pondering, thinking to myself, "Hmmm. I wonder what *that* means." I didn't own a childcare business, nor did I have any childcare clients. However, my kids were both in part-time daycare programs.

I wanted to take action on the intuitive voice that spoke to me. I went home and got online that same afternoon. After a few searches and clicks, I landed on a website called DaycareHotline.com that said it was for sale. A guy named Matt owned the online business, and it made money by selling start-up business plans and daycare forms to wannabe daycare owners and existing childcare business owners. It helped people get their daycare licensed by their state and gave them some tips on running a successful business. I thought "Cool! I'm a mom who has kids in daycare. And I'm a business and marketing pro. I can help these people (mostly women) start and grow their business!"

I instantly emailed Matt and asked him for more information on his online business. I wanted to know the price and more about its revenue and performance.

The key takeaway here is that I got a strong feeling and I took action on it *right away*. I followed my intuition immediately and kept following it with certainty to see where it would take me. This practice is called "following your feeling." In fact, this phrase comes from my spiritual mentor, Amir Zoghi. I didn't know it back then, but I got an intuitional "hit" or download from my higher self in that yoga class. And then I had the courage to take action, or to follow my feeling, by getting online and putting action behind it.

I bet you've followed your feeling many times. You got an inner certainty or knowing, and you stuck with it no matter where it led you, because you just knew it was right. It was honest and true. You trusted your process. Maybe you did so unconsciously, or you were aware that you had gotten an intuitional pull.

One well-known example of following your feeling in business is Jeff Bezos. Whether or not you're a fan of Bezos or Amazon, it's hard not to admire how he followed his feeling. Bezos left his successful career on Wall Street and moved to the West Coast with his wife to start Amazon—based on following his feeling. He famously wrote the business plan in the car during the drive westward with his wife at the wheel. Fast forward 25 years, and

Amazon is one of the largest companies in the world, and Bezos one of the world's wealthiest men. What if he had stuck it out on Wall Street because he was afraid to take the leap? What if he did NOT follow his feeling?

But how does following your feeling act as antidote to fear? Well, when you follow your feeling, you back yourself. The voice inside your head might be questioning a decision and making you feel quite nervous or fearful. But your "bigger self" carries you forward into the unknown, because you have a sort of sixth sense that it's the right path, and it's all going to work out. Even if it doesn't, you will learn a valuable lesson. This sixth sense is your intuition, your gut instinct. All of us have felt this at one time or another. But have you ever felt it and not trusted it? Usually when this happens, it's because of fear.

When I made the decision that day to follow my feeling, it set my life on a trajectory unlike any other decision I've made before or since. I said yes to a feeling, even though I had no idea where it would lead.

BOLTS...AND NUTS!?

At the moment I heard the voice speak to me on the yoga mat, I was working at the bolt factory in downtown Cleveland. It was my family-owned business, being run by my brother and co-owned by my dad and brother. I worked there three days a week since I had two little kids. I wore two "hats" at the bolt factory—Director of Marketing and Quality Assurance Manager. As you might imagine, the factory was extremely dirty and full of engine oil, and very loud. It was required to wear protective eyewear on the factory floor and a good idea to wear earplugs!

How in the world did my family end up in the bolt-making world of manufacturing with very little to no experience? Were we nuts? Well, in 1999, my dad—always the dealmaker—found a company for sale in downtown Cleveland that seemed like a steal of a deal at the time called The Auto Bolt & Nut Company. It was a classic manufacturing plant, forming rods of steel into bolts, and it had been around for over 50 years. But the glory days of this kind of business were far gone. Most of this kind of work went to China, where they can produce standard bolts and hardware for much cheaper than U.S. factories.

However, my dad felt there was an opportunity. I guess you could say he followed his feeling. He bought the business with my brother, and we all worked together for the next seven years to turn it around. I worked there from 2003 to 2009 and helped the company land on the INC 5000 List of Fastest Growing Companies. Today, Auto Bolt is the eight-figure business my dad always dreamed of. In fact, it has grown 20x from about $1.5 million in revenue to over $22 million in revenue today thanks to the hard work of my brother, Rob, who still leads the company as CEO.

One of the big ways we turned it around was to focus on "specials." These are very intricate bolts with detailed blueprints that require special tooling. These bolts might be used for things like windmills, John Deere tractors, golf carts, or other specialty applications. We knew this kind of work would not be likely to go to China or overseas. Plus, some of these customers required parts that were Made In the USA. This was our sweet spot! So, we went to work marketing and selling to these kinds of customers by going to industry trade shows, running ads in trade publications, and improving our online presence.

These were the very early days of the Internet, so I learned a lot about online marketing and lead generation through my job at Auto Bolt. I loved the power that the Internet gave to marketers. I was on fire, working on our brand awareness and making connections at trade shows. It was mostly fun to work with my brother, although as many siblings do, we could butt heads from time to time.

While I loved the flexibility of the job and the people I worked with, I wasn't really happy.

I longed to create my own company, or just do my own thing instead of spending my talents helping my brother with HIS thing. I wanted to make a difference for others and shine my entrepreneurial light. My gut told me that I had what it took to carve my own path to success. Or at the very least I needed to go out on my own and give it a really good shot.

I followed my feeling and purchased the DaycareHotline.com website business from Matt for $15,000. It was only generating about $1,500 a month in revenue, but at least it was something I could build upon. I calculated that in less than a year, I'd make my investment back. I figured I could use online advertising and content to attract more website visitors and buyers, and as I said, I knew how to market and sell. I had solid skills that could help daycare owners and wanna-be entrepreneurs.

However, I faced big fears around this decision. I was the primary breadwinner in my home with two young children. My husband had been hurt in a work accident and was home collecting workers comp pay. How was I going to make the leap from working at the bolt factory to starting my own business while still feeding my family? What if I failed?

I also had massive fears around what people would think. I'd never owned a daycare business. I just wanted to help women create successful businesses. What if I was seen as a fraud or imposter?

Then I remembered what my dad had always said, to focus on VALUE.

In fact, throughout my business journey, whenever I've hit a wall or faced fears about business growth (such as learning about a new competitor), I always ask myself about *value*, and I'll ask you these same questions...

- ► What is the true Unique Value that your customers or clients get from your business?
- ► Are you and your team doing the best job possible delivering value?
- ► Are there new/other potential customers in the market who would love the value you deliver? Do they know you exist?
- ► How can you add MORE value to what you currently do?
- ► What pent-up need in the marketplace could bring you more revenue and clients?

In this example, it was really helpful to support my "following the feeling" instinct with some practical business strategy. Back to the conversation I had with my dad in the car at age 13, what would help me Get and Keep Customers for my new business? What came up for me is to BE DIFFERENT. To figure out how my new business could be unique and have its own voice. I needed to create more unique value to offer clients. I'll dive further into this in the next chapter.

MY BIG A-HA MOMENT

Much later, I finally had this big realization—*no wonder* I had been searching for a business idea in my late thirties to build something great. The influences and childhood experiences from both sets of my grandparents—and both of my parents— were all around me! The adults who were my biggest influences were literally ALL business owners, and their blood was truly flowing inside me.

At the age of 40, working in the bolt factory, I had been prepped my whole life to build and own a business of my own. Yet, until that point, I was seemingly content to work for others. But the desire to be an entrepreneur was deep inside me, yearning to come out and be born. It was sitting in the formless energy, just waiting to be formed.

That was when I got the knock on the door at the age of 40, laying on the yoga mat that day in the spring of 2007. Saying YES to that knock was one of the best decisions of my life. Quite simply, I followed my feeling. My intuition knew it was there to be acted upon. So, I did.

Still, fear could have stopped me cold. Massive fears were in my belly and my mind as I was researching and considering how to move forward.

- ► How could I make enough money to support my family?
- ► What would my family say?
- ► Was I good enough?
- ► Could I balance the hard work it would take with being a mom?
- ► What if I failed?

◄ EXERCISE ►
Antidote To Fear #1: Follow Your Feeling

Can you recall a time when you followed your "Feeling" or intuition? Describe it in detail.

How did *following your feeling* help you conquer any fears that you faced? (*Check all that apply*)

- ☐ It helped me feel more confident
- ☐ It helped me stay calm as I knew it was the right path
- ☐ It helped me feel powerful
- ☐ It helped me be creative, more in the "flow"
- ☐ It helped me stay present

What are signs you can be aware of for the future with regard to following your feeling?

"How do you eat an elephant?
One bite at a time."

DESMOND TUTU

CHAPTER TWO

DO IT AFRAID

I n July 2007, I incorporated my business and became the proud new owner of DaycareHotline.com. My core strategy was to triple revenue in the first year by selling more start-up kits and offering a new monthly membership program. I wanted to build a community.

I followed the model built by online business coaches I saw in other niches—such as dentists, real estate agents, chiropractors, and mortgage brokers. The monthly membership would include a content-rich newsletter and a live monthly training call with Q&A from my members. I also interviewed an expert in the daycare industry every month and included an "Ask The Expert" audio CD of the interview in the newsletter mailing.

I had not yet quit my job at the bolt factory. This new venture was my "side hustle." I needed the steady income of my real job until I was making enough with Daycare Hotline to allow me to quit and go all in.

This is an important lesson. Take pressure off yourself whenever possible when you are building something new. Yes, I had to work evenings and weekends on the side business, so I had less free time. But I was able to meet the needs of my family and pay my mortgage without the pressure of needing the new business to make money. This gave me precious time to research, study, learn, and test new things, **to grow the business the right way and build a great foundation**.

In the meantime, I was living and breathing the world of online marketing, membership programs, business coaching, and high-end mastermind programs. *What's a mastermind program, you might be wondering?* A mastermind program is a group of people with a common goal, usually led by a mentor or facilitator.

I joined a local one right away so I could experience how it worked. I saw this as a smart investment! I was modeling what worked for others, in other niches, as fast as I could. I set to work studying other online marketers, subscription models, and everything about the childcare industry that I could find.

The cool part was NO ONE that I could find was creating what I wanted to build for the childcare/daycare owners who I wanted to serve. And my goal was clear: All I needed to do was generate $5,000 a month in income to be able to quit my day job at the bolt factory.

Those were the wild west days of online marketing, and it was a really exciting time. One of the best assets of DaycareHotline when I bought it was that it came up #1 on Google for the search term "how to start a daycare." It was getting 15,000-20,000 unique visitors per MONTH. This was a very high level of organic traffic at that time, which gave me lots of potential to grow the business. With the internet still in relative infancy, buying and selling stuff online was just gaining traction. Amazon had only been in business a few years, and social media was still called "social networking." A lot of people didn't trust it—yet.

Studying my new target market empowered me. I spent countless hours in the evenings after the kids were in bed, looking at other niche marketers and other daycare websites. Talking to my prospective clients empowered me because strategic ideas started to click into place and I could feel a shift of momentum swinging in my direction.

My typical routine was:

- ► **6 am:** Wake up
- ► Get kids up and dressed and fed
- ► **7 am:** Drive the brutal 1-hour commute to the bolt factory in stop-and-go traffic
- ► **8 am – 4 pm:** Work at the bolt factory (Hubby took kids to daycare)
- ► **4 pm:** Drive the 1-hour commute home and be happy if it took 45 minutes
- ► **5 pm:** Pick up kids at daycare
- ► **5:30 pm:** Make dinner, eat, baths for kids, TV time
- ► **9:00 pm:** Start working on Daycare business
- ► **Midnight:** Pass out in bed
- ► **Next day:** REPEAT!

Everyone who starts a business from scratch is familiar with the grind. But most of us are so empowered by creating something that's ours, we don't care about the exhaustion or the stress. We just keep taking baby steps of action.

That was one of the big keys to keeping my fear at bay—taking action so I could keep feeling empowered. During that time, there were many nights I could not sleep and many days when I was wracked with self-doubt. I recall one specific time when I was doing competitive research and found another site selling daycare business resources for a much cheaper price than I was. I questioned my strategy and became fearful that I was overestimating my value to the market. In fact, my then-husband Devin was questioning my whole situation! He said, "Oh no, we're doomed! That competitor is totally lowballing us. We should never have bought this business!"

At that moment, I resolved to keep going and not let fear—or my husband's fear—stop me in my tracks. I made a wholehearted decision that I could "do it afraid," but I had to keep going. *Don't quit.*

Reflecting back, there were three really crucial things I did in the first year I was in business, and these can apply to any start-up or any business that needs a fresh approach to growth... here they are.

BIG THING #1: CREATE A MASTER SPREADSHEET OF BUSINESS METRICS (KPI'S)

From my past work experience as a business analyst and marketer, I knew I needed a simple master sheet of all my business metrics in one place. Another word for metrics is KPI's, or key performance indicators.

If you're not familiar with the term "Key Performance Indicators," it's just a fancy way to say important numbers that help you determine how your business is performing. Some examples are top-line revenue, profit, key expense categories vs budget, new customer leads, new clients gained, customer or staff turnover—those kinds of things.

I created my Master Spreadsheet with months in columns across the top, and all my KPI's—key performance indicators—in rows down the side. (You can find my actual metrics spreadsheet in the Appendix in the back of the book). From revenue to web traffic to specific product sales figures, it's all there. I started with the basics and added on as I got more sophisticated.

At the end of every month, I entered all the data points for the business. I never missed a month. This allowed me to analyze the data and *slice and dice* it so I could understand trends, see the results of my efforts, and address any issues. It was my bible. It gave me CLARITY.

Admittedly, I love numbers. Working with business metrics and understanding my "marketing math" is one of my biggest strengths, and something I've done my entire career, even when

I worked for others. However, many folks who I've coached are not like me. They avoid numbers like the plague. If this is you, here's my guidance: you've GOT to understand the simple math of your business. It will help you see what's really going on in the business. It will give you the same clarity it gave me about what direction to take to grow.

This is where FEAR comes in. Fear comes from the unknown. From not knowing what to do because you have confusion or lack clarity. Practices like creating your KPI Spreadsheet will not only make your efforts to find more great clients and customers SO much easier—they will help you stay out of Fear-Mode. Not only will you save money on growing your business, you will grow your revenue so much faster when you know your KPI's, and you will do so with Confidence, rather than out of Fear.

Put it this way: no entrepreneur ever got to seven figures and stayed there for the long term without knowing their KPI's. If this is not a strength for you, find someone on your team or an outsourced pro who can do this for you each and every month. Then spend time understanding and taking action on what the data is telling you.

BIG THING #2: BUILD A MAILING LIST OF CLIENTS AND PROSPECTS (AND USE IT)

From studying other online marketers and coaches, I could see that the most successful ones all had lead magnets on their home pages. A lead magnet can be anything that is irresistible to your target audience, usually in the form of a free newsletter, video series, e-book, white paper—you get the idea. They were asking people to opt in via a web form to get the lead magnet.

For example, if your target market is moms, you might create a kids activity booklet, a cooking with kids recipe book, or a parenting video series. Anything that ties in to your expertise, sets you apart, and appeals to your ideal client.

The whole point of creating a lead magnet is to get people to opt in and build your list. Ideally, you'll be collecting names, emails, phone numbers. You might even offer something shipped to them, so you can get their physical mailing address.

My first lead magnet was a white paper called "18 Big Mistakes to Avoid When Starting Your Home Daycare." It was pretty popular among my website visitors. I was always tracking conversion numbers, so I could understand what percent of people were "opting in" for my lead magnet—and in this case, about 22% of them did in the first year.

After about 18 months of owning DaycareHotline, I had built an email list of about 1,200 subscribers. Not too shabby! This enabled me to consistently email my list and build a relationship with them. I emailed great content, sprinkled in with special offers to get them to join my monthly membership or buy one of my products or trainings.

This really helped me stay out of fear and have an asset I could leverage. Any time I needed a little cash, I held a sale with some holiday or even my kids' birthday as the reason, and I could make a couple grand almost overnight.

Any business owner can and should be building their list. This also has value when it's time to go sell your company.

BIG THING #3: WRITE COPY THAT APPEALS TO YOUR TARGET MARKET

No matter what kind of business owner you are, or aspire to be, you will achieve your goals much faster if you can get decent at writing copy. Copy on your website, in social media posts and ads, and in your newsletters for customers—these all are ways that people will experience the value you have to offer. You will make a connection with your audience, even if it's tiny.

Part of my intensive market research was studying the copy that people were writing. I studied headlines on websites. I looked at the copy of my competitors. I devoured books on great copy-writing. One of the world's best copywriters is Dan S. Kennedy, and I became his devoted student (you'll learn more about the impact Dan had on my life in the next chapter).

One of the big things I learned is that *words matter*. For example, I learned that some of my daycare clients did not love the word DAYCARE. They felt it cheapened what they did. They preferred childcare or early childhood education. I paid attention to these nuances in language among my target clients.

I also tested different approaches to copy. I learned about the power of an attention-grabbing headline on a home page, a lead magnet, or an email subject line. The point is to use copy to draw in your reader, and that starts with a compelling headline. My bold copy started to get noticed by people in the industry. I was hearing feedback and gaining a following. "Who is this Kris Murray person and where did he come from?" Yes, some folks thought I was a man when they first discovered me. That never bothered me. I just wanted to become known and make a difference.

These three things were all strategies I did before I quit the bolt factory. They were part of the important foundation I was build-ing.

TRULY UNDERSTAND YOUR BEST CUSTOMER

Here's the thing. I was starting to learn that the clients who bought daycare start-up kits and forms from me at Daycare-

Hotline.com were VERY price-sensitive. And it was hard to get them to "stick" inside my membership community. You might say they were kinda "flaky." It felt like they were either unable to invest in their at-home daycare business, or they were too busy watching the kids to really care about their own growth.

After owning DaycareHotline for a year or so, I realized I needed to go spend time with my actual target customers if I wanted to grow my business. I learned about all the national, state, and local conferences being offered to childcare owners and leaders—so THIS is where they all hung out! I got my husband to agree to watch the kids so I could go to my first leaders conference—the NACCP event—being held that year in Orlando. The year was 2008.

(What was going on in 2008 in the United States? Well, the beginning of the Great Recession. I'll talk about how the recession actually HELPED me later on.)

I had a HUGE epiphany after I went to the Orlando trade show. I met all sorts of daycare center owners and attended some conference sessions. Most of these owners had "brick and mortar" centers, many owned their real estate, they served from 200 to 1000 children each day, and they had MUCH deeper pockets than my DaycareHotline client base did! They were spending money on conferences, travel, curriculum, staffing, leadership, rugs, and furniture—all sorts of things! The vendors at these shows seemed very happy, serving great clients and making money!

And one MORE big a-ha... literally NONE of the conference sessions were about anything business-related. They were all trainings about the daycare stuff: child development, playtime learning, brain studies, state licensing, music, and art. Which is great, we need that too, of course. But where was the BUSINESS content? The marketing, staffing, financials, operations, enrollment? How did they know how to run a successful business? Literally zero percent of this conference was teaching that stuff.

I talked to owners at lunch and happy hour and asked them my question regarding business content. Some looked at me with blank stares. But some responded with a "YES, we really need that! That would be so awesome to have a conference that's more focused on helping us grow our business!"

Which brings me to perhaps the most important nugget of this entire book: when you get an idea for a business, and you can see a pent-up need for it but it DOES NOT EXIST YET, you've really got something. Say nothing to no other humans and go directly to your desk and start building it. Immediately.

And that's exactly what I did.

I acknowledged the fear, but I kept going. I took "baby steps" of action and always stayed in momentum. And I did it with wet pants. But I did not stop.

◄ EXERCISE ►
Antidote To Fear #2: Do It Afraid

Can you recall a time when you took a leap of faith to do something big, or take an important step, even though you were afraid? Describe it in detail.

In the scenario above, what resulted from your decision to go ahead and *"do it afraid"*? (*Check all that apply*)

- ☐ It helped me realize the fear was an illusion
- ☐ It made me more confident the next time I faced a big leap
- ☐ It helped me trust myself more
- ☐ It made my heart happy, and I felt lighter
- ☐ Other: _____

Do you resonate with the analogy of "doing it with wet pants" and if so, how?

"A leader is one who knows the way, goes the way, and shows the way."

JOHN C. MAXWELL

CHAPTER THREE

FIND YOUR TRIBE

I brought home some momentum from that Orlando conference. I decided I would build a true business coaching system, or online program, for the daycare owners who already owned centers. I could also start modifying my monthly membership program to appeal to these folks.

This decision was based on the massive realization that people who owned brick and mortar childcare centers and preschools were going to be better clients for me (in general) than the home daycare providers I was serving. They had deeper pockets and were more business-oriented. For example, the husband-wife team that owned my kids' child care center, TLC Academy in Hudson, Ohio. These fine folks were named Alison and Kent Pfeister and they changed my life.

My kids had been enrolled at TLC for a couple years when I had a conversation with Alison about the work I was doing. I told her I was creating business content and strategies for childcare centers to grow their enrollment, especially at this difficult time in our economy. As parents were facing layoffs, the first thing to get cut in the family budget was daycare.

This meant that thousands of childcare owners were starting to feel the pinch. Alison was no different. Her center held a max of 110 children, and six months into the recession she was sitting at just 55 kids or so on her roster. She was barely covering expenses.

Alison was very interested in hiring me as a consultant to help her with her marketing and help her attract more kids and families. She made me an offer I could not refuse.

She said, "If you work for me as a consultant part-time and help me get full again, I'll give you free tuition for your two children."

I did the math in my head. We were spending about $1,800/month on childcare at that time. Needless to say, I instantly accepted her offer! Not only could we save money for our family, I could use Alison and Kent's business as a "test case" for my methods.

I got to work examining TLC's website, their search traffic and leads from new families, and how many tours and enrollments they were getting. Then I came up with a marketing plan for how to increase their leads and enrollments. More about this to come.

At this point, it was now May 2009. I was balancing three days a week at the bolt factory, working with Alison as a consultant, and continuing to build my business at DaycareHotline. Plus raising two kids. One day, I was on a jog after work, blowing off steam. All of a sudden as I was jogging across the bridge on the way home, it hit me like a ton of bricks. Last month I had a net revenue of about $4,700. I was *so close* to my goal of $5,000 a month, I could taste it!

At that very moment, I felt the truth land in my heart. It was time to quit the bolt factory. I was going to work solely for myself.

MY FIRST BIG WIN

Now it was time to really get serious. My next revenue goal was clear: get the business to 6 figures. Double it to $10K a month, and things could really start taking off. I spent the summer of

2009 creating new products for my clarified target client—the brick-and-mortar daycare center owner. Again, these were the type of people I talked to at that conference, and they were the people who owned my kids' daycare.

I did the research. There were about 45,000 of these owners in the United States. A good size market that no one was serving with business content or seminars.

By the fall of 2009, I had an updated website and a new online information product for this group. It was called The Child Care Business Success System and I created two versions. A Silver version for $697 and a Gold version for $997.

I kept a cold bottle of Veuve Cliquot champagne in the fridge awaiting my first online sale of this much higher-priced product. Remember, I was used to selling daycare kits and forms in the range of ten to 30 bucks. So, these new products were designed to take my revenue to the next level, and they also had a lot more in-depth business content in them.

I'll never forget the moment my email inbox lit up with my first order. Bing! "You've got an order for $697." A little shriek of joy erupted from inside me. I ran downstairs and opened the fridge, grabbing the champagne. I ran outside to the backyard where my husband was playing with the kids on the swing set. "I GOT MY FIRST SALE!"

Champagne never tasted so good.

With this first success in hand, I was hooked. I started promoting and marketing myself like crazy to the daycare owners in Ohio and then all over the United States wherever I could. I went to state conferences and "schlepped" my products as a trade show booth sponsor. I did workshop sessions as a conference speaker which set me up as an expert to the audience.

In 2010, I created another product called "Enrollment Bootcamp." This was a 5-week online training course that I did "live" with people via online classes. (Nowadays we use Zoom but it didn't exist back then, so I used GoToWebinar). People signed up from around the United States and even internationally. I was teaching owners how to double or triple their preschool's enrollment, and they were getting huge results from what I was teaching them! My name started to become known little by little among my target customers. In one memorable conference workshop, my session was standing room only to a group of childcare owners in Georgia. That day, when I made my pitch at the end of the workshop, I made a whopping $13,000! I hit a home run and could barely wait to get home to process all the orders.

As I've mentioned, daycares all across the U.S. were still feeling the effects from the so-called Great Recession. They were desperate to try anything to grow their enrollment. My Enrollment Bootcamp actually got them results, and because of those real results, I benefitted from positive word of mouth across the industry. The recession—as bad as it was in some ways—was a boon to the growth of my business.

THE PERFECT DAY EXERCISE

As I was following various internet marketers to keep learning and growing, I stumbled across Frank Kern. Frank was a force – his strategically crafted marketing concepts, delivered with a self-deprecating charm and hilarious wit, had made him tens of millions of dollars in various niches, including dog training courses of all things. He was doing a webinar on how he manifested his dream life and wanted to teach us his secrets. Of course, I could not resist attending.

The core content of Frank's webinar that day was called The Perfect Day Exercise. The core question was: If there were no limitations or consequences, what would your perfect average day look like? He guided us through a detailed process to get in touch mentally and emotionally with our ideal, regular, perfect day. Here's the questions he asked us:

- ► What time do you wake up?
- ► What do you have for breakfast?
- ► Where do you live?
- ► What's your home like?
- ► What car do you drive?
- ► Who do you spend your early morning with?
- ► What do you do for work?
- ► What are your work hours?
- ► What's your work space or office look like and where is it located?
- ► What value do you deliver with your work, and for whom?
- ► Where do you eat lunch? What do you eat?
- ► What's your financial situation? How much money are you making?
- ► What's your family life like? Are you married, and if so, what's your partner like?
- ► What do you eat for dinner? Who cooked the meal?
- ► What are your evening activities?
- ► What kind of places do you like to travel and how often?

And so forth. The idea was to really tap into what we loved. What would make us truly happy, fulfilled, and feeling utterly ALIVE? What was the lifestyle we were yearning for in our deepest hearts' desire? Maybe even things we didn't dare admit to ourselves because they seemed so outlandish, impossible, or even greedy. At the end of the exercise, my vision was clear. I wanted to be doing the work I was doing, building the company of my dreams and serving the child care industry. I wanted a luxury mountain home in Colorado, on a river. I wanted two vehicles: an Audi SUV and a Porsche 911. I wanted to be able to afford household help, like a personal assistant and a housekeeper. I wanted fun experiences with my husband and two children, and several high-end vacations a year.

Frank then had us estimate the budget it was going to take to afford each of these things. I figured I could live my dream life if I brought home about $35,000 a month. That seemed within my grasp. I made a plan for how I was going to achieve that revenue and profit margin. As you'll see, it only took me about two and a half years into being a business owner to hit that number.

This exercise really ignited something inside of me. I decided to teach it at my very first Child Care Success Summit event in 2012. I took the audience of 150 folks through it, step by step, just like Frank did for me.

Jennifer Conner was in the audience at that Summit. She had received my infamous "bank bag" mailer in which I mailed a sales letter to attend the Summit to about 500 owners around the country, inside an actual bank bag. It was a big success. Anyways, Jen was *all* in, when I taught the "Perfect Day" exercise from stage. She diligently wrote down everything she felt would make her regular day, a perfect day. Her experience was so profound, that she later taught the exercise on main stage to our Academy members.

A key component of Jen's perfect day back then was to live in New Orleans, and grow her child care brand to be the best in her community. Later, she dreamed of owning a condo in Mexico and running her preschools remotely from the beach. And that's exactly what manifested for her, after she started working with me as her coach in 2012. (Jen then became my Director of Coaching in 2019 and ultimately stepped into my role as CEO of our company in 2023. More about that later).

In 2020, I bought my luxury dream home on the river in Colorado. I still own it today, and enjoy that river every day. I also bought a white Audi Q8 SUV that year.

It took eleven years after I did the Perfect Day exercise until I felt abundant enough to buy my dream car – a Porsche 911. My family was full of Porsche fans. My dad had owned a 911, and my grandma owned a 928 back in the eighties.

I was at a mastermind meeting with The Trust, in Scottsdale. The Trust is a group of 7- and 8-figure women, led by Ali Brown. The ladies and I were out to dinner the first night of the retreat, and the cocktails were flowing. I said, "I was searching up the Porsche 911 inventory here in Scottsdale, and there's a metallic blue baby at the dealer that's calling me. But I should probably wait until I get back to Colorado to really start looking."

They were all over me. "Go get that car!" they all said. "You've been talking about it for months!" "What the heck are you waiting for?!"

I wanted to pay for my dream car in cash. Writing that check in the Porsche dealership was one of the most powerful things I ever did. The dealer was full of "bro's" who were wheeling and dealing. And in I waltzed, blonde hair and flowy outfit with heels, pointed at the car, took the test drive, and wrote the check. That was a good fucking day.

If you need inspiration to keep reading, this part is for you. I want you to know that whatever your heart truly desires—whatever you love—can be yours. You just need to *activate the aligned energy and follow your feeling*. Our bodies are made up of neutrons, protons, and electrons. We **are** energy. It's not woo-woo, it's science. It may take a decade to show up, but then again – it might show up for you tomorrow. You just need to believe that it's happening, and make a whole-hearted decision. I'll share more about this process later in the book.

A LOCAL MASTERMIND GROUP

Throughout this period, I was growing the business pretty consistently and I could taste the seeds of possibility. Still, there were doubts and fears in my mind and in my belly. My biggest issue was trying to balance being a mom of two young children with the big dreams I had for the business. Many days, I felt like I was giving neither job the attention it deserved. Even more difficult, people close to me in my life still didn't believe I could pull it off.

I remember one holiday dinner with my extended family where I was trying to share my baby steps of success. The men at the table—my stepdad and my brother most notably—pretty much ignored me. They didn't think a business helping daycares was legit. They probably saw childcare as many still do— "glorified babysitters." This fueled my burning desire to prove them wrong. I needed to prove to all the naysayers that I could be successful. This is another valuable takeaway if you're just getting started—ignore the negative nellies.

I knew that it was important to surround myself with a tribe of people who could support my positive mindset. I searched for a community of people led by a mentor who knew the ins and outs of businesses like mine. Luckily, I found a local mastermind group that was the perfect fit—and pretty affordable—about a 40-minute drive from me.

I joined this group in early 2010 right as I was creating the Enrollment Bootcamp course. My new tribe helped me launch the course successfully and think bigger about how I could grow the business. A game-changing step for business coaches like me was to do live events and seminars. This was a daunting idea. I'd have to book a hotel or meeting space, market the event, and fill it with child care owners. People would have to travel to come see me speak. Talk about "doing it with wet pants!"

This tribe of about 20 online business coaches (in all different niches) led by a mentor really helped me stay out of fear-land. As I started to get little wins and celebrate my successes, my confidence began to grow. Having this community was a great antidote to my fear. And remember, I had only been on my own as an entrepreneur for about eight months at this point.

Another little toe-nibbler of fear was the stats about business start-ups who fail. It's a fact that only one out of three new start-ups succeed after three years. And only 14% of female-owned businesses ever break the $500,000 mark in revenue. Yikes! I had to just put my head down, keep implementing good ideas, work hard, and refuse to quit.

MY FIRST EVENT: ENROLLMENT BOOTCAMP LIVE

I'd heard about the strategy of creating a "Pre-Conference Event" by booking a space in the same city as another industry event. In other words, hook your event onto the front of another larger event that people were already traveling to. So, I created a one-day seminar the day before the 2010 NAEYC conference in Anaheim, California that child care leaders could attend one day prior to the conference. NAEYC was (and still is) the largest child care conference in the U.S. with about 10,000 attendees.

Dan Cricks was the guy who led our mastermind group in Cleveland. He was SO excited for me to take the huge leap and do this event. Even though it was just a 1-day seminar hosted in a rinky-dink little hotel conference room, it was a big step for me! I felt scared and excited all at the same time. I think I charged something like $397 for the day, and it included lunch and a fun group dinner at an Italian restaurant.

I marketed the event with many emails to my list, plus a post-card mailer to people who I had addresses for. I didn't have a lot of money for marketing, but I tried to make an impact with the funds I had.

The event took place in mid-November 2010, and I was thrilled to get about 12 people to attend. I presented content all day, had the participants do workshop-style exercises, and share their experiences with each other. We had a great time at dinner. I felt a sense of fulfillment and encouragement that I was on the right path and making a difference. Even if it was just 12 people, it was a solid start.

The next day, I set up my booth for the big NAEYC conference. I figured I could give away some cool swag, build my list of prospects, and maybe even sell some stuff. The thing I didn't realize is that this event draws mostly teachers and educators, not owners and administrators. So, there were very few of my target clients at this show. I ended up selling just a couple courses and mostly giving away free stuff to teachers.

Dinner with Enrollment Bootcamp Guests (not all were able to attend)

But I didn't see it as a loss. Even though I **spent** more money than I made while in California, I talked to as many people as possible at NAEYC, and I continued to learn a ton about my audience. The networking was awesome. Similar to my experience in Orlando, I realized there was a need for a BUSINESS-focused conference in this niche. Ideas were forming in my head for how to create a multi-day event to help child care owners with their business and leadership skills.

"LITTLE HINGES SWING BIG DOORS"

At this point in my journey, I could sense there was a big door that was about to swing wide open. The key was to find the little hinges that could be the levers for that to happen. I continued to seek out mentors and tribes of like-minded people that could help me find those hinges.

Dan Kennedy was the guy who probably made me aware of most of those levers, and had the biggest impact on me over the lifetime of being an entrepreneur. I met Dan in 2006, way before I got going in business. His ideas and strategic thinking consistently blew my mind. Two of Dan's biggest platforms were the books he wrote and the seminars/events he led. He also swore by creating your own "media"—being the author of your own monthly newsletter.

Following his advice, I already had the newsletter thing going, along with the CD of the month. At this point it was 2011, and I had about 75 clients paying me 50 bucks a month for the newsletter membership. This was a great cashflow strategy—consistent income that laid the foundation to pay all the bills each month so I didn't have to go out and hunt for my next dollar. This definitely helped me sleep better at night.

Dan often said the best clients he had—the ones that paid the most and stayed the longest—came from his books. They spent hours and hours of time with him through reading his ideas, which eventually turned them into clients. This nugget of wisdom really stuck with me. I knew the next little hinge I needed to swing: become an author.

I had a bunch of decent content from writing my newsletter and creating courses. I just needed to figure out the purpose of the book, create a solid outline, and organize the content to make it flow. Another one of Dan Kennedy's most powerful platforms was the idea of "Market-Message-Media match": getting the right marketing message to the right target market using the right media. I was inspired by this idea. So, I created a similar framework for my book, but I included "metrics" as well. Here's a picture of the 4 Pillars that were the foundation of my book:

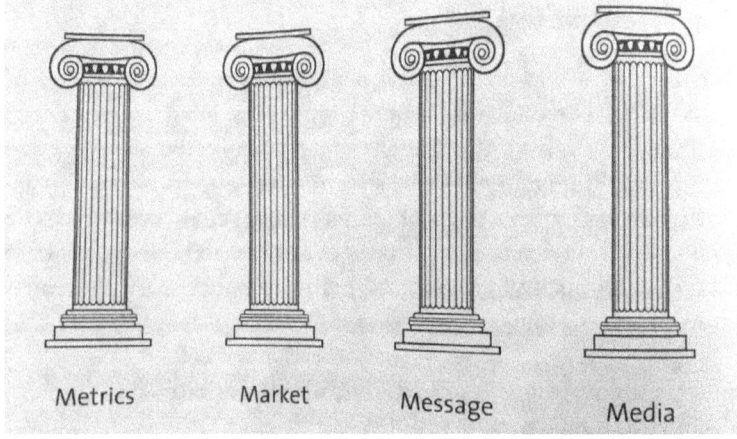

Metrics   Market   Message   Media

Four Pillars of Effective Marketing

I decided to call the book *The Ultimate Child Care Marketing Guide.*

To my delight, the book concept was picked up by a child care industry publisher and I got a publishing deal with Redleaf Press! They gave me an editor and agreed to feature the book in their catalog, which was mailed to thousands of child care leaders each month. This was going to be a great way to get my name and my book in front of my target audience!

There was just one problem—it was almost impossible for me to get the book done in the middle of my chaotic life. My children were my first priority. At the tender ages of five and eight-years-old, they demanded so much of my time. On top of that, with all the content creation, product delivery, client relationships, marketing, and administrative tasks, the business was growing super-fast and I could barely keep up.

I had an idea. I saw a workshop called "Write Your Book in a Weekend" led by a writing coach. The idea was to sequester myself off somewhere for the weekend and just write my ass off. The writing coach would hold me and the other workshop participants accountable and inspire us to keep going. My then-hubby was very supportive of the idea. And my mom's beautiful home was vacant, as she and my stepdad were away in Florida. I moved into her house for the weekend, stocked myself up with food and snacks, and got writing.

Once again, I used a community of like-minded people led by a coach to support my goals and keep fear at bay.

After hundreds of hours and many edits, my book released in January 2012. When I held the first copy in my hands, tears came to my eyes. I was so proud. It might sound corny, but it felt like I had birthed another baby.

Just like Dan Kennedy had experienced, being an author catapulted me to another level. Large enterprise-level clients (like Childcare Network with over 200 locations, as well as Primrose Schools) started talking to me about consulting gigs. My list of prospects continued to grow and my monthly revenue was climbing.

◄ EXERCISE ►
Antidote To Fear #3: Find Your Tribe

Have you ever joined a peer group or mastermind group? If so, what was the main reason you joined?

_____

_____

_____

_____

_____

_____

_____

_____

_____

_____

_____

How did *finding your tribe* help you conquer any fears that you faced? (*Check all that apply*)

    ☐ It gave me a sounding board for help and advice

    ☐ It helped me avoid costly or painful mistakes

    ☐ It made me feel more supported

    ☐ I received content, ideas, or coaching that helped me

    ☐ It helped me realize that mistakes are a natural part of growth and learning

Reflect on your experiences in peer group(s). What did you learn that sets the stage for future growth or future groups you might want to join?

"To be yourself in a world that is constantly trying to make you something else is the greatest accomplishment."

RALPH WALDO EMERSON

CHAPTER FOUR

HARNESS YOUR EGO

I t was the spring of 2012. My book was gaining readership and getting great reviews. My business was on track to do nearly $600,000 in revenue for the year, so it was doubling or tripling in growth every year since it launched in 2009. I was intensely focused on revenue and profit and very data-driven from the beginning. (To see a chart of my actual revenue growth over the history of the business, check out page 180 in the Appendix).

Many business owners, especially the ones I was working with in the child care field, are not naturally data-driven. They resist looking at and understanding the math of their business. If this is you, it's totally understandable to want to grow your business by "feel" or gut instinct rather than by the numbers. You may also see the focus on numbers or money as being driven by ego—or greed.

I didn't see it that way. I knew the only way I was going to scale my company was to be able to hire a team so I could start delegating. And the only way to afford a team—even just one employee—was to be profitable. To get there, I had to be intensely focused on the monthly revenue and expenses.

At this point, I was definitely the bottleneck of the business. I was doing all the things. Just a few months earlier, I had hosted another conference-style event. This time, it was a two-day event at a nice Sheraton hotel near the Cleveland airport. I really went *all in* on this event. And after months of intensive marketing, including direct mail letters and online advertising, I got 52 people to fly or drive to Cleveland—not the sexiest of destinations!—to join me for two days as I hosted this seminar.

Consider this accomplishment for a moment. Just the year prior, my audience size was *twelve* women. I quadrupled it to 52 people this time. I covered all my costs for the event and made some extra. And the most exciting part was, this was the first time I was going to offer high-end coaching to the audience.

I had studied models for coaching programs far and wide, so I could understand what other coaches were offering and what fees they charged. I really weighed out the pros and cons of all the options. Some people offered in person events in cool locations, versus "virtual only." Another big consideration was length of commitment. Did I want to require a year membership, or let people go month to month?

I decided to go big or go home. Charge more, make it an annual program, and really deliver results for people. Include in-person mastermind events at attractive places like Clearwater Beach, Florida, or Boulder, Colorado. Back to the Cleveland event, on the first afternoon of that seminar, I pitched my new mastermind concept: Kris Murray's Platinum coaching program, exclusively for child care business owners. It took real courage to stand on that stage and charge $8,000 for an annual mastermind program that had no track record. Some would say, it took a bit of ego as well.

A BIG EGO? OR IMPOSTER SYNDROME?

A lot of my childhood was spent around people with big egos. When I was a little kid, I naturally didn't know what the ego was or how it could show up. When I got a little older, I began noticing comments about it; stuff like "he's such a show off" or "what a braggart." I don't want to talk badly about my dad at this point, but he could be a real egomaniac at times. I was embarrassed about his show-off behaviors, especially in front of my friends.

I came to realize later that my dad—as well as other "big ego" people—probably felt insecure deep down inside and he used his ego to hide this fear. He figured that if he bragged about his latest success, it would impress people. That way, people wouldn't discover his flaws, weaknesses, or insecurities.

When I stood on that stage and offered the $8,000 annual program, it was a huge leap for me. It required me to see myself as someone who had valuable gifts to offer. **If I didn't believe I could do it, no one else was going to.** So yes, I guess that required me to dive into my ego in order to protect my self-concept. If I didn't, I was going to be seen as a fraud. I would suffer from imposter syndrome so severely that I would risk gaining no clients and being a complete failure.

Keep in mind that I was a marketing consultant and a mom who was attempting to start the first ever high-end coaching program for daycare business owners, yet I had never owned my own daycare! This would be equivalent to someone teaching dentists how to build their practice, who had never been a dentist. Possible but definitely not easy! This potentially damning storyline was in the back of my head, reminding me from time to time of what people might think of me—that they might see me as a fraud.

BOLD MOVES AHEAD

That first year, I got six clients who said Yes to the Platinum coaching program. Woo-hoo! I was on my way to building a successful coaching business. I included one-on-one coaching calls, group calls, tools and templates, and three in-person mastermind retreats in the Platinum Program that first year. As I mentioned earlier, we chose fun locations for the retreats: Clearwater Beach in January, New York City in May, and Boulder, Colorado in August. The group was really starting to gel and get great results for their preschool businesses.

2012 was also a big year of changes in my personal life. My husband and I had been dreaming of leaving the Midwest and moving the kids back to Colorado, ideally to a mountain town where we could raise them with a love of the outdoors and nature. Devin was a Colorado native and we'd been plotting this move for the past few years. A big part of our strategy was to be able to work for ourselves and make enough income to support the family, so we could live wherever we wanted.

Devin and I had actually met in Denver and that's where we got married and had our first child, Owen. Then we moved the kids back to my hometown of Hudson, Ohio (near Cleveland) before my daughter was born. We wanted to be close to extended family to raise the kids. But in time, we realized that being in Cleveland was not our ideal. Even though we launched the business there, and it was great to be near family, we just weren't that happy with living in Ohio. Our dream was to get back to the mountains. We just really, really missed the West.

After considering lots of choices like Steamboat Springs and Park City, we landed on our ideal place—Crested Butte, Colorado. Crested Butte is a tiny little town of 1500 people at the end of the road in one of the most gorgeous spots in Colorado and as I'll share in the next chapter, I had lived there once before, in my twenties in the mid-1990s. We loved the charming town, the vibrant community, a good school for the kids, and the bonus was a very cool ski resort.

This was our chance to have a new start, create a new "dream life" in a ski town, and run our business from there. We plotted out how much income we needed to live there, and what neighborhood we wanted to live in. This move would prove to be the launching off point for the next phase of the business and my life.

It was the middle of June 2012 when we put the house on the market in Ohio and loaded all of our stuff into a U-Haul. We had sold a bunch of stuff, including most of our furniture in a massive yard sale, and three days later, we took everything that remained that we wanted to keep, and headed west. I drove our one vehicle, the Subaru, with the dog and the kids in tow. My husband drove the U-Haul, and off we went on our merry way with our caravan across the country. Our dream was within reach. With the business mainly being on the internet, we could live and work virtually anywhere we wanted, and we wanted the mountain life for us and our kids.

I'll never forget the feeling in my heart when we arrived with the U-Haul to Crested Butte. It felt super surreal to be back in this place that I loved so much. My heart was overflowing with joy and happiness. We picked up the keys to our beautiful furnished rental home and hired a couple of local kids to help us unload the U-Haul. The next day, I bought a pair of shiny new skis from a sale that was taking place at the local ski shop. I was on cloud nine.

DISCOVER YOUR STRENGTHS

After we got settled, it was time to work on the business. We determined what each of our strengths were, and we dove into expanding them. (Even though we've parted, my ex was my business partner, and I have to say that he really helped me get to our first million). His strengths were the technical side and the digital marketing. He was helping our clients with improving their child care websites as well as making sure ours ran smoothly. He was running Google Ad accounts for clients and for us as well. Back in those days, social media wasn't nearly as big as it is now. But we helped clients get comfortable with it.

They were asking things like, "What is Facebook and should I have it? Should my childcare center have a presence on there? How do I get started with that, and how do I make good content posts? Do I need to learn how to make videos?" Devin was learning all the building blocks to help clients market their preschools online. Anytime we needed to make a landing page or make a change to our website, he took care of it.

On the other hand, my strengths were being the "face" of the business and doing the coaching. I was really good at helping clients become more data driven, figure out how to solve issues, and implement strategies to grow. We determined our core brilliances, so we would try to *not* step on each other's toes. As a husband-and-wife team, it is always challenging to try to make sure that you don't micromanage each other, or you don't get in each other's way or get into fights about who does what. We put some good thought into that.

Most business owners, when they start, they're wearing all the hats, and the goal is to take the hats off one at a time. "I don't need this hat. This guy's going to take that hat." My husband wore his half of the hats, and I wore the other half. Eventually, little by little, we were able to say, "Okay, this hat belongs to a social media person or an admin and I can start to move away from those tasks." That's the process. If you write an organizational chart, even for yourself or one or two of you, then you can't say, "Well, you did my work, or you didn't do your work." It's all right there, right in front of you. I'm a big fan of business structure and organization—charting and defining the roles of each person in the company. It really helps keep things on track.

Things were going pretty smoothly. The next big step we took was to find an office because we quickly realized that things were way too cramped working out of the home office together. The ideal would be an office space in town, close to the kids' school, big enough for three desks—one for each of us plus a third if and when we needed to hire an assistant. We were lucky to find a great fit, an affordable office in walking distance to the school!

The kids started walking to the office after school, where we had an iPad for homework and a TV with headphones, with a couple of bean bags set up for them. We could manage things with them and still be in the office working. This arrangement worked out really well, and things were going pretty smoothly in balancing parenthood and CEO duties.

HIRING OUR FIRST EMPLOYEE

The office set up also enabled us to hire our first employee—a huge and exciting next step! Her name was Camille St. Martin, and we hired her for 15 to 20 hours a week, part time. It was a nice stepping stone to be able to do this because it was affordable. We hired her as our office manager as well as administrative assistant.

It was fabulous to have somebody who we could start delegating tasks to. She could do some social media, handle the office administration, order the office supplies—all of those more clerical, administrative type duties that neither Devin nor I had time for. As she began to know more about the clients and our voices, she did some writing for the newsletter and the blog. She was a great all-around hire and she was super speedy in most of her tasks. I was like "Damn, I should have done this a long time ago!"

It can be super scary to hire more staff when you don't know how you're going to afford it. But then after you do it, a light bulb goes off. I realized that taking that kind of leap of faith is what enabled me to continue to grow. There will be stuff that you don't want to do and should not have to do, and learning that your time is much more valuable in one area than it is in another is when you really begin to see growth. This is a valuable lesson that every business owner needs to live through to truly learn. I call these types of lessons "trusting the process."

A great way to get your mindset right about hiring is to ask yourself: What is my time worth? Do I want to spend my valuable time on a task that drains me, or can I could pay someone $15 to $25 an hour to do that dreaded task? If my time is worth $100 an hour, am I mostly doing $100 an hour work? You've got to really look in the mirror and hold yourself accountable to delegating the stuff you hate, that drains you, or that's below your pay grade.

THE UNIQUE BRILLIANCE EXERCISE

To that point, one of the pivotal tools that I use to this day to help me in this area is called The Unique Brilliance Exercise. This is the exact tool I used back in 2013 to help me figure out what to write in Camille's job description, before I hired her.

The Unique Brilliance Worksheet has been hands-down one of the most important and powerful tools that I've used for myself, as well as for my clients.

It's set up in quadrants. Basically, you put the tasks and type of work that you LOVE, that energizes you, and that you're good at, in the top two quadrants. Then you put the things that you're either really bad at, that you HATE, or that drain you, in the bottom two quadrants. I have a template for it, and we use it all the time. We still use it today with all the businesses in the coaching that we do, and it helps you get a list of specific tasks, responsibilities, and duties that you're going to give to the person when it's time to delegate those things.

I actually still have the one from 2013 that I used when I hired Camille. Here's a picture of it. The idea is if you focus on the tasks and projects in your work that give you energy and that

Unique Brilliance Exercise

you love, you're going to be way happier. You'll be in the flow, build your business faster, and make a lot more money because you're focused on your unique brilliances. Then you let go of everything else, you delegate everything else.

I've got to give credit to two of my business coaches for this tool. The first is Dan Sullivan, the founder of Strategic Coach and the "wet pants" guy. Dan created this tool, and he calls it the Unique Ability tool. Another coach I worked with that taught me to use this tool is Fabienne Frederickson. Fabienne and her mastermind group really helped me grow during this time in my life. I was in her coaching group from 2011 to 2013. Thanks to both Dan and Fabienne for sharing this amazing tool with me and holding me accountable to really apply it, so I can now share it with you.

IT'S AN INVESTMENT, NOT AN EXPENSE

One more key point needs to be said here. When you hire to delegate the stuff you should not be doing, you are making an investment in yourself and the future of your business. **It's not an expense.** I know it can be scary to spend money on scaling your team when you feel like you can't afford it. You say to yourself, "Why spend that money when I could just do it myself?" Right? But while you're doing those low-level tasks, what else could you be doing that would bring in a lot more business? You can't be penny wise and pound foolish.

Another thing that happens to business owners is that they start to panic. "Well, how am I going to come up with an extra $100 or more every week?" If you pay a person for four hours work at $25 an hour, you will spend $100 on them, yes. But if you're making $200 an hour or even $100 an hour, do the math. **The time you would have been doing those tasks you delegated, you could have been getting new clients, doing the high-value work that only you can do, and growing your company.**

HOW EGO KEEPS YOU AFRAID

During this pivotal time in my life as my business was approaching a million dollars in revenue, my ego was playing a bigger and bigger role. I was getting really well known in the child-care industry and I wanted that success. My ego was driving me forward because it wanted that recognition. But the shadow side of the ego is that it wants to keep you safe and in your comfort zone. It felt like a double-edged sword. It was saying, "Get out there because people are loving what you're doing. You're becoming a huge success!" But also it was wanting to keep me small. Can you relate?

Harnessing your ego isn't easy. Here I was like, "Oh, I wrote a book, I'm on stage and I'm traveling in first class, and look at 'fancy me.'" But the other side of the coin was that my ego didn't want me to leave my comfort zone. For you, that might look like avoiding marketing and sales to keep your client load small. Or not wanting to have too many employees, so you can keep your payroll costs down. You tell yourself it's okay to play small, that big isn't necessarily better. Maybe it's a limiting belief that people are going to come after you or think you're a big shot. That's the part of the ego that wants to keep you safe and in check.

So how do you start harnessing your ego? You can start simply by *being aware* of when you are in ego. The ego is looking for recognition, appreciation, approval, acceptance, or security. As my mentor Amir Zoghi says, "It's looking for love in all the wrong places." Ego can keep you in fear because you care so much about what other people think—you're looking for false love in the external world. The key to harnessing your ego is to reclaim your own power back to your own heart and your truth. You truly stop caring what others think because you spend time on your own self-worth and deservingness. You become more aware of when you're "in lack" or in a fear-based mindset. Like many other mindset habits, it's just an awareness practice.

THE ANTIDOTE TO FEAR

So many people are afraid of their true power, of their ability to have this limitless, incredible business, and so they stay intentionally small because **they're afraid to really shine their light**. Shining their light can feel too bright, and it scares them. This is how the harnessing of your ego can be an antidote to fear. Ego actually keeps you small, and it can keep you in a place of fear because you don't want your infiniteness to shine. It's too scary.

◄ **EXERCISE** ►
Antidote To Fear #4: Harness Your Ego

Can you recall a time when you acted out of ego, because you were looking for recognition, acceptance, approval, or safety? Describe it in detail.

_____

_____

_____

_____

_____

_____

_____

_____

_____

_____

_____

_____

How did *harnessing your ego* help you conquer any fears that you faced? (*Check all that apply*)

- ☐ It helped me reclaim my power back to myself
- ☐ It helped me feel more calm and centered
- ☐ It helped me care less about what others think
- ☐ It helped me feel less judgmental about myself or others
- ☐ It helped me stay present
- ☐ Anything else? _____

What signs you can be aware of for the future with regard to acting out of ego, and then harnessing your ego?

Harness Your Ego

*"Become the person your future
thanks you for and forgive the
past for the mistakes it made."*

SETH GODIN

CHAPTER FIVE

EMBRACE THE HARDSHIPS

B y 2014, things were really humming along in my life and my business. Living each day in my dream mountain town of Crested Butte, Colorado, was awesome. That was the second time in my life that I lived in Crested Butte (locals refer to it as CB for short). The first time was when I was in my twenties, from 1992 to 1997. It was a pivotal time in my life because I discovered my love of nature, spending time in some pretty hardcore mountains at 9,000 feet elevation. I became an expert skier and a skilled mountain biker while working for the ski resort running their market research program.

Now, many years later, life was really good. Being able to come back to this community that I felt was truly "home" in my heart was so fulfilling, and being able to raise kids here was extra special.

The kids were doing pretty well in school and making friends. We moved the office to a larger space, just one block away from our home. It was the best commute on the planet! Every day we sent the kids off to school on their bikes (or on the bus in the winter) and then I packed up my work backpack with laptop, and off I walked the block and a half to the office, with my dog Simba in tow. Pretty great.

My team and I were able to take the Platinum Coaching program and add two more levels to it—a starter level for smaller business owners called Gold Membership, and a deluxe program with more bells and whistles for large multi-site owners called

THE ANTIDOTE TO FEAR

Platinum Plus. The program overall had close to 75 clients in it—up from the **six** we had that first year! We were on track to hit a million dollars in revenue.

My husband was helping me in the business and things were going fairly smoothly for us at home. Of course, we would have arguments from time to time about the issues in the business. Unfortunately, those fights often occurred in front of the kids either at the dinner table or in the kitchen.

"The website got hacked. It keeps going down. I think some dudes in Asia are the culprits. I don't know how to keep them from hacking us!" said my husband in major frustration and stress.

His "lane" continued to be the tech side of the business while I continued to be the face of the business, the main coach, and the growth strategist.

"Sorry, honey. Just keep trying to fix it. That's all we can do, right?" I probably wasn't much help to him, although I tried to be sympathetic.

It seemed like 2014 was a year of so many issues and problems as our business was approaching seven figures. It was often difficult and frustrating for us to juggle all the work situations while maintaining a good marriage and being solid parents. The business began to put a strain on our relationship, and the cracks were really starting to show.

At that point, we had two full-time employees and were considering adding a third. We had an Operations Manager, a Junior Coach, and were looking to add a Client Support Specialist. The team was performing pretty well, especially considering it was a blend of in-person employees who came to our office, and remote team members who worked in other states.

MY SECOND BOOK: 77 BEST STRATEGIES

The first book, which had come out in 2012 and really catapulted my personal brand as well as the business, was doing well, but it had one problem. It was technically "owned" by my publisher, so I couldn't get inexpensive copies of the book to sell at trade shows or to offer in the back of the room after my stage appearances. I needed to self-publish a smaller book focused on "tips and tricks" so I could get books into hundreds of hands of potential clients for a lower out-of-pocket cost.

The answer: self-publish my own book using Amazon and Kindle, and have it printed on demand. Writing that book was a big focus for me in the Spring and Summer of 2014. I leveraged blog posts and other content I had already written, which is a great strategy to re-use content you've already got. That fall, I launched my second book. It was called "The 77 Best Strategies to Grow Your Early Childhood Business." It sold like hotcakes and the strategy was a winner. I was able to order books for just over two bucks apiece and either sell them at events for $10-$15, or give them away for free as gifts to potential clients.

I was in yet another "mastermind" group of peers with business coaches at that point. It was called War Room, led by marketing powerhouses Ryan Deiss and Frank Kern. You probably remember Frank's name from the "Perfect Day" exercise. As I've said, Frank was an online marketing genius who I admired and modeled as much as I could. It's worth repeating—modeling the ideas and actions of others who are more successful than you is a HUGE strategy that I used very intentionally to grow fast. And in 2014, we were on target to make our first million bucks just five years after I quit the bolt factory. The business was doing better than I could ever have imagined back in 2009 when I sold that first online course.

Frank Kern ran a famous promotion where he sold his latest book for One Dollar. It was wicked smart. Get people to pull out their credit card to buy a book for free plus one dollar for shipping. Then upsell them into a variety of one-time exclusive offers that were super hard to resist. Frank probably made a million bucks just from that one promotion. I was paying close attention.

So, what did I do? I ran the same exact promotion, but switched it up in some ways to "make it my own". (I always recommend *modeling* successful people, but be sure not to COPY them directly because that's copyright infringement). First, I sold the book for $5.60. That's the flat USPS shipping rate for a small package like my book. Then I did the One Dollar promotion like Frank did. Sure, we'd take a loss on every sale. But we upsold people to various courses and memberships off the back of that promotion. I got a lot of new customers that way and was able to get hundreds more people reading my book and getting to know me.

That promotion was a massive game changer for me. And it helped me stay out of a fear-based mindset because things were working. My confidence kept growing as the business grew and we gained more and more leads and clients.

I took the results of that promotion as a case study to share at the War Room mastermind retreat in Vegas that year. I even got to hang out with Frank Kern in the green room of the event. I was meeting my mentors and influencers, and it felt very empowering. I knew I was on the right track.

VEGAS, BABY!

Having attended the War Room retreat in Las Vegas, we were drawn to the excitement of that city as a possible location for our own events. I was working with an individual event coordinator named Nancy Kludt and she happened to have a connection to the managers inside the Luxor Hotel on the Vegas Strip—you know, the hotel shaped like the Pyramids of Egypt. So, we said,

"Hell Yeah, let's take the Child Care Success Summit to Vegas," and we signed the hotel agreement with the Luxor.

The 2014 Summit conference was another massive gamechanger and "upleveling" of the business. Lots of new potential clients attended, and the audience size grew to a new all-time high of 450 people.

Another uplevel was our new team of MCs (Masters of Ceremony). These guys called themselves the Bungalow Boys, a group of three aspiring actors and video production guys from Atlanta. I had met them at the Georgia state childcare conference where they were the MCs. They were incredibly fun and dynamic on stage. I thought to myself, *I gotta have these guys MC my show; they will bring the house down!* They were super handsome young guys, so I knew that my mostly-female audience would go nuts for them. I asked them if they'd travel to Vegas to work my event and their answer was a resounding "yes!"

I got a new wardrobe for the event and so did my husband. We wanted to not only feel the part but look the part. We broadened the event agenda to include some powerhouse speakers, and our big sponsor partner was Care.com. We interviewed the co-founder and CEO of Care on our stage and that was a huge "get" for us. It really legitimized us to the audience and the world.

That was a core strategy I learned from my various mentors over the years. Surround yourself with celebrities and well-known experts from your niche, and the audience will start to view YOU as the expert, too. You can become an influencer just by getting other influencers to create content with you or appear live with you—even if you have to pay them.

By this point, we had a robust exhibit hall full of sponsors and booths—about 30 companies paid us to be in that hall. That was another great strategy. The event was largely subsidized by the funds we got from sponsors. We had to market the event to fill it up, get those butts in the seats, as they say. But the sponsors were happy to have a spot in the hall and they mostly did very well selling their products and services to the attendees. The energy was electric and everyone was having a great time. I mean, hey, it's Vegas, baby! What could go wrong?

FIRE ALARM HELL

Since my main stage keynote speakers were of higher caliber this time (Dennis Vicars and Danny Morris, two well-known experts in the child care field), I wanted everything to be perfect for their sessions. Dennis was first and he was fantastic. The audience was in rapt attention to his every word, and I could not be happier. Remember, the strategy here is that impressed audiences buy more and sign up for high-end coaching!

Danny was onstage later that day. In the middle of his talk, all of a sudden, the hotel fire alarms went off and boy were they LOUD. Like, ear-deafening loud. Everyone put their fingers in their ears, and some people left the ballroom. Danny just stood there, attempting to talk on his mic but no one could hear a word he said. I was mortified. I ran to Nancy in helpless panic, and she said there was nothing she could do. I'm like "Huh? Get on the horn to your buddies in the management office! Do something!!" She said something about this being a typical fire alarm "malfunction" and that it was relatively normal. I could not accept that. After all, I was spending hundreds of thousands of dollars hosting this event.

At that moment, I faced fear head on. All the panicky thoughts ran through my brain. What if people leave and never come back? They could easily be lured away by the casinos which are right downstairs! What if my reputation is ruined? What will future speakers think? Most importantly, I was going to pitch my high-end coaching programs the next day. Would I even have an audience to pitch them to?

I had to take several deep breaths and try to calm down. I embraced the hardship and tried to find the silver lining. We could use this calamity to band together and get a big laugh from the audience. We could overcome the hardship together as a community. The fire alarm finally stopped, the audience came back, and the event went onward.

The next morning, the inconceivable happened. Once again, the fire alarm went off in the middle of a keynote session. I was absolutely beside myself! And once again, I got no help or advice from the hotel staff or my event manager, Nancy. As I consider myself the utmost professional, this situation was completely unacceptable to me. But I was stuck. I had no control and could only ride the waves of fear, anger, and helplessness that I felt.

Later that day, the most important sessions of the entire conference were slated to happen: the Success Panel and the Pitch. The idea was to get a handful of successful clients out on stage with me and ask them questions designed to showcase how working with me has changed their life and made them so much more successful—and wealthier. That's the Success Panel. Then I'd flow into offering our coaching packages and make a direct pitch to everyone in the audience to join.

The entire time I was on that stage during that all-important session I felt like my armpits and palms were sweating all over the stage. I was SO stressed out just waiting for that damn fire alarm to go off! It was like my life was in slow motion and every word had my baited breath hanging on it. Well, luck was finally in my corner. The alarms did not go off. I got through my pitch with flying colors. And we got a whole new large crowd of folks come to the back table and sign up. We got enough sign-up forms in Vegas to get us close to our first million dollars in revenue. We headed back home to Colorado, exhausted but happy.

TROUBLE ON THE HORIZON

As my husband and I continued to have success, we also continued to struggle in our marriage. I kept trying to smooth things over, but it felt like the threads that held us together were getting very close to breaking.

One night in late December of 2014, my husband Devin and I had a massive blowout. The intense argument caused him to say, "Fine! Then I will hand in my resignation, and you can grow this business alone." He went to the office late that night, typed up his formal resignation, stomped back into the house in the middle of a snowstorm, and handed it to me with great drama. It was official: I was alone as the CEO and owner of the business, and it was now my sole responsibility to grow it.

Secretly, I was overjoyed.

I began the morning "commute" of the block and a half to work on my own. I sat in my office and reflected on the relative silence. I had two other employees in the office at that point and we each had our own separate spaces, so it was a really calm and peaceful vibe in there. I started to feel the spaciousness of running the business solo, and I loved the energy of that space. As the winter months of 2015 transitioned to springtime, I had a huge realization: I wanted space in my romantic life as well. I wanted to be single and free.

Devin and I took the kids on Spring Break in mid-April that year. We went to Longboat Key Beach, Florida—a common destination since my parents lived in Sarasota. My mom would get early access to our condo and stock the fridge and pantry with all our favorite food and cocktail ingredients. It was a delightful, relaxing vacation—except that I was falling out of love with my husband. He was not working and kept asking me what he should do next for his career. At that point, I didn't really care what he did. It might seem unkind, but I had spent so many years trying to smooth things over and keep his self-esteem propped up that I was fucking exhausted. I wanted "me time." I wanted to take the kids and create a new life. That vacation was the first time I uttered the words to my mother. "Mom, I'm thinking about getting separated from Devin. I'm unhappy." She nodded and seemed to empathize with my situation. But I believe that in her heart she knew it was going to be a long and painful road ahead for me, regardless of which path I chose.

NECKER ISLAND

During that time, I had several business mentors who'd been invited to go to Necker Island, Richard Branson's famously beautiful private island in the British Virgin Islands of the Caribbean. It was a bucket list trip for both me and Devin. We idolized Richard and were huge fans of the companies he's built. Earlier that year, we'd gotten a random email from a buddy in the War Room mastermind group that a couple spots had opened up for a Necker Island trip with a bunch of fellow entrepreneurs. We jumped at the chance.

In May of 2015, we flew to Puerto Rico, then to a tiny island in the Caribbean. From there, we took a power boat to Necker. We were greeted by the staff on the beach with champagne. I felt like I just landed on Fantasy Island.

We had four amazing nights there and stayed in the main house. Everything on Necker is decorated in Balinese style, with flowing white fabrics and dark wood furniture. It was super luxurious, and the food was outstanding. We got to hang out for several meals with Richard, and we were part of a small group Q&A session with him. I asked him a question which he answered, but I have no memory of what I asked. I was quite starstruck and just soaked up every part of that experience.

Richard is an avid kite-boarder and the team was offering kite-board lessons down at the beach one of the days. Devin signed up for that, but I wasn't too keen. I was down near the activity on the beach when I spotted an empty golf cart with the key in it. Always the risk-taker and a rule-bender, I jumped into the golf cart and went up to the main house. I got a beer from the fridge and took off for a joyride around Necker Island. The island features a natural habitat for several species of animals, including lemurs and 50-year-old giant tortoises. I visited both that day on my self-guided golf cart tour. (To this day, I love driving golf carts and purchased my own suped-up cart with a light-up sound bar that sits in my garage).

Being a "mermaid" on Necker Island

I feel that this might be a valuable lesson for someone reading this who wants to take more risks but is stuck by fears of what others think. I am SO happy I took that golf cart. No one minded, and no one judged me. I experienced the ultimate feeling of FREEDOM during that afternoon ride. So go ahead, do the thing. **Live life to the fullest with no regrets.**

One other really memorable experience on Necker was a mermaid photo session that was organized for the ladies on the trip. A professional mermaid-style swimmer was there to give us lessons in underwater swimming, along with an underwater photographer. We'd been told that this was taking place, prior to the trip—so if we wanted to be a part of it, we needed to purchase a mermaid tail of some type and have it shipped to the island. Mine was a beautiful sequin blue. I have photos and video of

me being a mermaid under the sea on Necker Island. I'll never forget the experiences I had there.

DIVORCE AND FULL CUSTODY

Despite our wonderful trip to Necker, Devin and I remained unhappy. We tried yet another therapist, this time an online one that would meet with us via video calls. It just wasn't working. In the summer of 2015, I knew it was over. I told Devin I wanted a divorce. He agreed to my request, although I could tell he was really hurting from my decision. He said we should tell the kids, so that next evening we did. As every divorced parent knows, this is one of the hardest things you'll ever do. The kids burst into tears at the news. After we told them, they ran to their rooms to cry and commiserate. They were 10 and 13 years old.

It took a year for the divorce to be final. We had gone through several rounds of mediation, then individual attorneys. The judge decided to award me full custody of the children. That was good news in one sense. I avoided the intense stress of co-parenting with someone who had great anger and hatred towards me, which would not have been healthy for the kids nor me.

But I was faced with another fear: how am I going to manage being the full-time single parent to these two teenagers, while growing a seven-figure business and managing a growing team of employees? Could I wear all the hats and stay sane? I had a pit in my stomach about what my life was going to be like. I just had to pull up my big girl panties and dive in, one day at a time.

FLAT ON THE MAT

Fast forward to March 2017. My life was in the shitter, and I didn't think I could face it. Two weeks prior, a trusted employee of mine sued me out of the blue for $850,000. The suit alleged wrongful employment practices that were not based in reality whatsoever. It would have been laughable if I hadn't been so heartbroken.

My 14-year-old son was in trouble with the local police and had been suspended from school. And to top it all off, I went out on St. Patty's Day to drown my sorrows and got a DUI. I had to spend a night in jail and sobbed all night behind bars.

I was flat on the mat—at an all-time low in my life. I had no more "positive mindset" to give and no one to help me through the mess. Hell, I didn't even have a driver's license! Due to the DUI, it was revoked for 90 days, even though it was the first time in my life I had ever been in any sort of trouble. Every day, I risked more jail time to drive my kids illegally to school. You see, there was no Uber or other options in my tiny town of Crested Butte, Colorado. And I was a full-time single mom of two teens.

In my business, things were close to collapsing. When my former employee left, I had to immediately hire a high-powered (read – expensive) attorney firm in Denver to fight the lawsuit. Then I had to take back the entire, rather large, client load that she had been covering, doubling the number of hours I had to spend on one-on-one coaching calls. I was cash- and time-strapped and had no earthly clue how much longer I could hold on. The day-to-day stress was almost unbearable.

All throughout that month of April 2017, I reflected on what had happened. How had I gotten here after things had been going so well? What personal responsibility did I have in how these events had played out? There were four key roles I was playing in my life and I needed to ponder and reflect about the truth in each of them:

1. My role as a single parent of my kids, now 14 and 11 years old

2. My role as a business owner and CEO, who needed to keep the business alive
3. My role as a divorced ex-wife and how I was dealing with my ex
4. My role as a coach and mentor to my clients, who would only stay with me if I could keep my reputation shiny and positive

I dug down DEEP that month and came up with a new mantra. I was going to hire an "army of coaches" and never again be dependent on one key employee in a pivotal role in the company. That dependence on ONE thing in the business was a killer. And I knew better. My early mentor Dan Kennedy had a famous saying: "The worst number in business is ONE." That means anything you have just ONE of is a kiss of death. One client. One system. One key employee. One method of payment. One person looking at your books.

You've got to scale to be able to have multiple people and systems for all the key areas of your business. That way you don't rely on ONE. And if that ONE leaves you or breaks down, it can mean the death of your company. (Dear reader, PLEASE take this advice to heart!!)

THREE NEW COACHES & THE RE-SET BUTTON

Once I had clarity about scaling the coaching lane of the business, I got to work QUICKLY. I asked myself who I could reach out to that would make an excellent part-time coach, and who was likely to want the job. It was only a matter of days before the answer showed up: Ben, Jennifer, and Brian. All three said yes, and we were on our way with a new era in the business, and a small army of coaches. Each of these coaches had been clients who I'd helped make outstanding gains in their businesses. They were each from a different geographic region, and they

had unique innate strengths and skill sets to bring to the role of coach.

The first quarterly client meeting with my three new coaches was in San Diego in May 2017. I remember vividly the moment I sat next to Jennifer in my San Diego hotel suite and talked about our strategy for the future. She said, "This is the moment we are hitting the Re-Set button, okay? We've got this." I wholeheartedly agreed. A new chapter was being written in that moment.

I settled the lawsuit with my former employee. We proved that the allegations were false and whittled the money all the way down from a demand of $850,000 to a settlement of $30,000. *That was the best check I ever wrote.* And it ties back to another famous quote from my mentor Dan Sullivan (the "wet pants" guy) who says, "If you can write a check to solve your problem, you don't have a problem." I wrote that settlement check as fast as I could and let the problem fade into the rearview window. I hit the re-set button and got my new coaches together for a retreat at the Colorado office after we came home from San Diego. We all masterminded together and crafted a new plan for the growth of the company.

Sometimes, your worst nightmares can actually be supportive for you. I look back on that moment, and I know now that those hardships were actually designed FOR me. It was supportive for me to see that I could actually get up off the mat and survive. I had to get hurt by that employee to harden my shell a little bit and become the true CEO that I needed to become to grow the company to its next level. And I could share the over-coming of hardship with my clients to inspire them and let them know they were not alone.

◄ EXERCISE ►
Antidote To Fear #5: Embrace the Hardships

What is one of the biggest challenges you've faced, and how did you overcome it?

_____

_____

_____

_____

_____

_____

_____

_____

_____

_____

_____

_____

_____

How did **overcoming that hardship** change you as a person? (*Check all that apply*)

- ☐ It made me more confident
- ☐ It gave me courage to face the next challenge
- ☐ It helped me feel powerful
- ☐ It increased my deservingness
- ☐ Other: _____

THE ANTIDOTE TO FEAR

Reflect on the times you've had challenges versus the times that felt easy. What insights can you gain about embracing any hardships you may face in the future?

With my dad on my wedding day

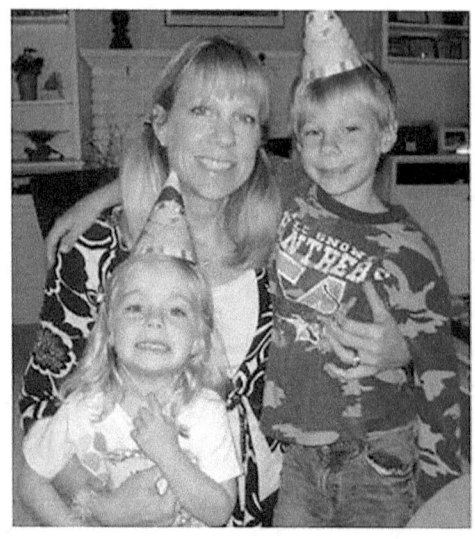

With my kids when I first got the idea to start a business

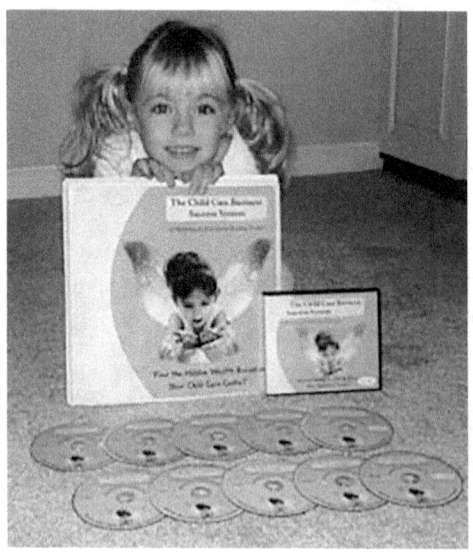

My daughter Maeve with my first big info product

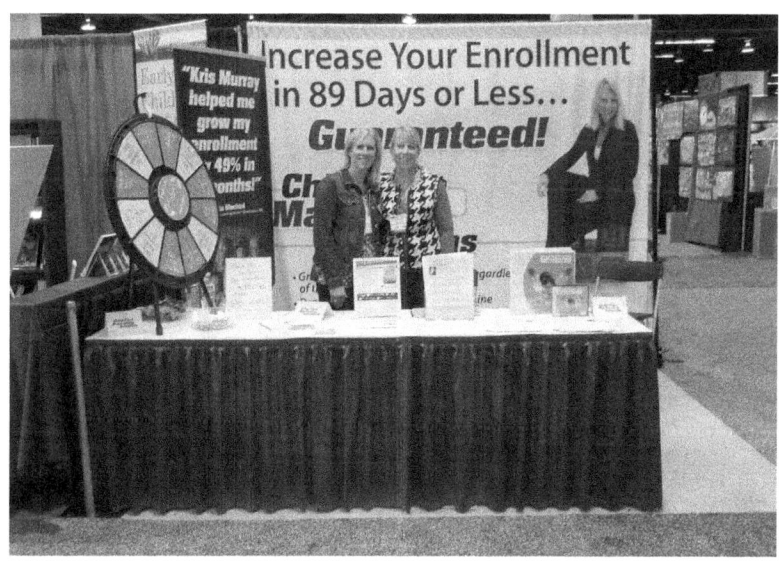

My exhibit booth at that first NAEYC conference

Connecting with wonderful clients was always meaningful

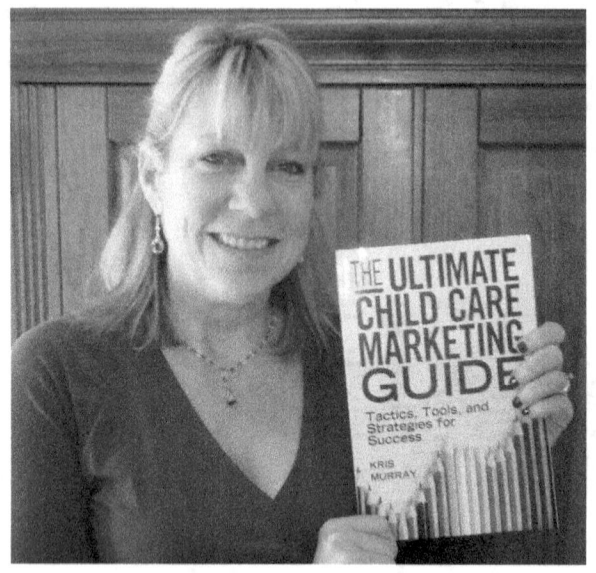

Proud of becoming an author

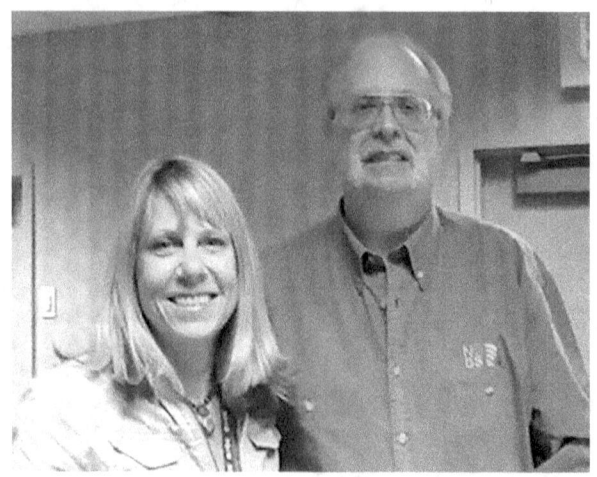

With my mentor Dan Kennedy

Early days hosting the Summit event (Vegas 2014)

Hosting my podcast in the Carbondale office

The day I got John Maxwell Certified as a Coach & Speaker

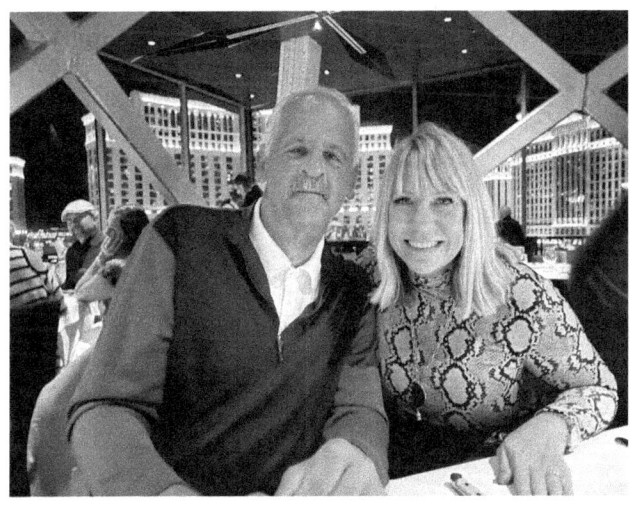

Me and Stedman Graham (Oprah's man)

The day I bought my dream car - Porsche 911

Me and my fabulous mentor Ali Brown

Me and Daymond John goofing around on stage

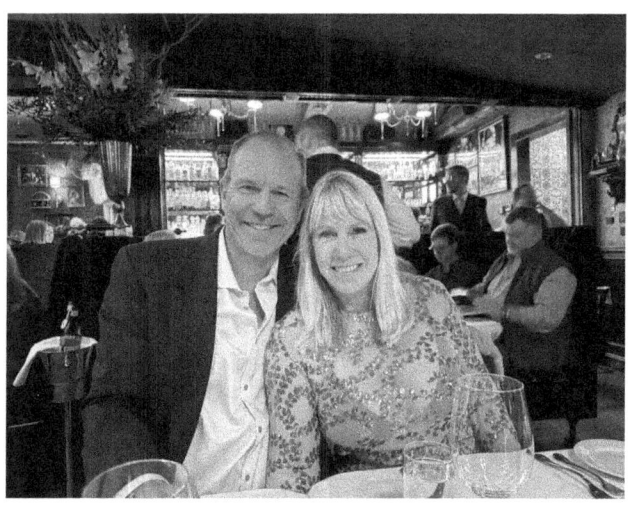

At dinner with my fiance Chris

"Life is either a daring adventure or nothing at all."

HELEN KELLER

CHAPTER SIX

SPEAK YOUR TRUTH

A fter the madness and stress of the DUI, my parenting challenges, and the restructuring of my team, I wanted to not only hit the re-set button in the business, but I wanted a fresh start in my personal life. I had been dating a man named Charlie for about 18 months, and it was a long- distance relationship. He lived in Glenwood Springs, a town two to three hours' drive from Crested Butte. We saw each other a couple times a month, and I felt it was time for one of us to move closer to the other one if we were really going to make a go of it. He had two boys the same ages as my kids, and I was also hoping he could be a positive role model for my son, who was still having challenges.

With my desire for a new beginning for me and my kids, I decided to make the move to a nearby town about 10 miles away from Glenwood Springs, called Carbondale, Colorado. It was a cool place, a little bigger than Crested Butte with a bit more social and arts happenings. And it was only 30 minutes from the ski mountains of Aspen and Snowmass—bonus! I found a super nice four-bedroom house with a big home office on the golf course. Once again, it was a furnished rental so we could just pack up our personal items like clothes and toys and make the move relatively easily.

As you might guess, at the ages of 15 and 12, the kids were not super jazzed about moving to a new school and having to leave their friends. I tried to be sympathetic and ease their transition as much as possible. I had been lonely in Crested Butte after the divorce and was feeling a lot of strain being the only adult caring for my two teenagers, plus dealing with the DUI ramifications (classes, community service, etc.). I needed a better support system, and I was hoping that the move to Carbondale would provide that for all three of us.

However, I did have to dig down deep and face some fears as a single mom of two teenagers during this time in my life. I was taking a huge leap of faith that moving away from our beloved town of Crested Butte and starting a new life two hours away would turn out positively. I was trusting the process and following my feeling. Still, I had some voices of doubt in the back of my head. As we packed the boxes and met the moving van, I was just praying that this move was going to work out for us.

THE BIRTH OF MY PODCAST

During the summer of 2017, I also observed that the most successful marketers and coaches were using the format of podcasting to get their voice out there. One that I followed quite closely was Ali Brown. Ali had a top-rated podcast with a huge following called Glambition Radio, and I loved her format. She mostly did interviews with successful entrepreneurial women, and then occasionally she'd do a solo episode covering an important idea or promoting something she was doing. It was incredibly successful and inspiring.

One of my great "loves" was being on the air. When I lived in Crested Butte during both the 20's and 40's phases of my life, I worked as a volunteer DJ for the local public radio station called KBUT. I absolutely loved it, and people told me I had a good radio voice. Since I already had a broadcasting background, and a pure love for creating audio content, I decided to create my own podcast. I called it Child Care Rockstar Radio and launched it in September 2017. Over time, my podcast developed a strong loyal audience. Most episodes gained 1,500 – 2,000 downloads and some even more. I had already found my voice creating content, courses, and videos for the childcare market. Now I had a new platform to further my reach and speak my truth even more clearly and passionately.

MATCH YOUR MARKET

As I mentioned, the old Platinum program from 2012 had now been expanded to three distinct levels of coaching to meet clients where they were. In 2018, we gave the Academy another facelift of sorts. We updated the names and benefits of each level to better match the aspirations and "avatars" of each type of client. The program now had levels known as Growth, Freedom, and Empire. This naming scheme and the improved benefits of each level more closely matched what the clients wanted, and it helped us sell more people into the program.

This is a big "writer downer" if you're reading this and trying to grow your business. The key strategy here is to Match Your Market. What do I mean by that? Once again, this is something I learned from ole Dan Kennedy. He taught us to make sure we had a Message to Market to Media match. For example, if you're a plumber, you're probably not going to spend gobs of money advertising in a luxury magazine for women. You'd be much smarter to focus your marketing dollars on local family-oriented newspapers and online apps like NextDoor, to laser target your offers.

We named our specific avatars so we could really go deep into their mindsets and paint the true picture of their pain points. Our new avatars were:

- ▶ **Solo Sally/Sam:** a single-site owner who's also in the manager seat, doing all the things herself and drowning.

- ► **Multiplier Mary/Mike:** a multi-site owner who's not in the manager seat but gets sucked back in and wants to scale her leadership team.
- ► **Empire Ellie/Ed:** a multi-site owner who wants fast growth to build an empire and a larger team—usually with deeper pockets.

Once we had our avatars and messaging in place to match these segments within our market, things really started to click. Growth from 2018 to 2020 was gangbusters and with the podcast in place and team growing, we felt unstoppable.

THE IMPORTANCE OF CORE VALUES

It was around this time that I sensed the company needed a deeper dive on setting the foundations of our culture. Through one of my mastermind groups, I became aware of an awesome book called *Built On Values* by Ann Rhoades. Ann had worked with companies famous for building great cultures, like Southwest Airlines. She actually helped the CEO of Southwest, Herb Kelleher, create the core values, and then gained the buy-in of the company's leaders, which is the critical step so they "live and breathe" the values—not just framed and hung on the wall. She did the same thing for JetBlue Airlines and lots of other companies, large and small.

It made a huge impact on me. There were about five of us working at the company at that point. I gathered us all together and we did an exercise following Ann's advice in the book. It said to get in front of a whiteboard or flip chart and have all your employees there, if possible. Then ask everyone to think about clients we serve and the work we do, but most importantly HOW we serve people. What adjectives come to mind that best describe the "vibe" of our little company, and how we do what we do?

Everyone just blurts out words that they are feeling fit us. The session leader (you) writes them down as they're being shared. Write down your own, too. There's no wrong answer and no editing at this point. Keep going until the list is exhausted. Then, ask everyone to choose the top three words or phrases that they love the most. The ones they really FEEL are right, from an energy perspective. Then make a tally. Everyone says their top three. Using hashmarks, which four or five words are the winners? (Southwest just had three: Warrior Spirit, Servant Heart, and Fun-Loving Attitude).

At the end of our core values process, we had five values in place: Outside the Box, Passion, Integrity, Impact, and Fun. We also had our clear "why": to impact one million children through improved childcare programs and leaders. We knew our clients were running more stable, successful businesses with better leadership and teacher teams in place. They were high quality programs, providing improved education for children. This "why" was extremely motivating for everyone on the team, and it gave us fuel to be all-in on growth.

A few months later, I was thrilled to see Ann Rhoades in person. She was presenting a live workshop session at a marketing conference I happened to be at. I went up to her after her talk and let her know I was a huge fan of her work. We had a wonderful conversation, and I just loved her energy. With that connection in place, it seemed only natural to invite Ann to come and speak as a main stage keynote speaker at the Child Care Success Summit. She did an amazing job, and the audience loved her. Later, I had Ann join me on my podcast. If you want to check it out, especially if you're interested in how to create a values-based culture for your company, she's on Episode 36 of Child Care Rockstar Radio.

SOCIAL PROOF

Another important thing I focused on during my entire journey is a thing called "social proof." It's the idea that **what other people say about you has been shown to be 17 to 20 times more credible than what you might say about yourself** in terms of promoting your business or your personal brand. My mentors were all huge advocates of using social proof—like reviews, testimonials, endorsements, and awards—to build their companies. After using it myself for years, **social proof has proven to be the most important component of my marketing message**. I am known for helping my clients get social proof from *their* clients (parents of young children) and put those video testimonials, written testimonials, and five-star reviews all over the internet.

My big quote that I say all the time is, "You simply cannot have too much social proof. Period." One of the tools that I teach clients is a checklist of all the places I like them to put their social proof messages—on their preschool vans, on signage out front, on their school's phone message, obviously on all their digital media, on team T-shirts, on the walls of their centers, and on and on. My checklist has 12 ideas for where to put these testimonials and reviews (see Appendix for the checklist). And it's one of the most powerful and effective strategies I've ever taught to *change the game* for my clients.

I intentionally used my podcast for social proof by interviewing clients who had inspiring and impressive success stories as a result of working with me in coaching. It was a subtle way to get this powerful testimony out there in the world in a big way. I asked my guests specifically designed questions on the podcast to share "what's working" in their business, so listeners can get real case studies and hear this proof first-hand. The podcast is a huge vehicle that still works to this day to attract more prospective clients to the business. Yep, Child Care Rockstar Radio is still cranking out new episodes twice a month as of the date this book was published. And like Ali Brown, I do occasional solo episodes to connect in a deeper way to the listener or viewer (it's also on YouTube) and cover a key topic in more depth. I also use it to promote important events and promotional offers to the audience.

Ali was also one of the key people I studied and learned from to create my high-ticket mastermind program back in 2012. She's known for teaching other women how to develop a platform using big stages and events to sell their programs and get their personal brand out there in a big way.

Ali (as well as Dan Kennedy) inspired me to create a big stage of my own. After I did the two-day event in Cleveland back in 2011, I was hooked on the power of creating my own conference event and using that to offer my coaching programs.

THE CHILD CARE SUCCESS SUMMIT

I used what I learned from Ali, Dan, and other mentors to create my signature event that is still running successfully to this day—the Child Care Success Summit. The first Summit was back in 2012 in Denver, and I attracted an audience of 150 childcare business owners. The Summit is a three-day event, carefully choreographed with a mix of celebrity speakers, great sessions, lots of fun and high energy, and an intentional invitation on the afternoon of Day Two to join our coaching program, now known as the Child Care Success Academy.

The growth of the Summit is one of the greatest accomplishments of my career. This timeline should demonstrate why my team and I are so proud. Very few event hosts can accomplish this:

2012: Denver, 150 attendees
2013: Atlanta, 300 attendees

2014: Las Vegas, 450 attendees
2015: Orlando, 600 attendees
2016: Phoenix, 750 attendees
2017: Chicago, 900 attendees
2018: Dallas, 1100 attendees
2019: Orlando, 1200 attendees—the peak
2020: Virtual Online, 1200 attendees
2021: Las Vegas, 1050 attendees
2022: Nashville, 1100 attendees
2023: Orlando, 1000 attendees
2024: Chicago, 900 attendees

As you can see, we moved this event around to key cities all over the U.S. This strategy works really well because we constantly attract new audiences who live within driving distance to the venue. For our clients, Orlando was probably the biggest draw because they used it as a business expense to bring their kids or grandkids with them and go to the theme parks. Or just get relaxing pool time.

The 2019 show was the peak of the event's attendance because after COVID, everything changed. People aren't traveling as much for work (in general), probably due to inflationary pressures. And for us, the competition in childcare business conferences has gotten more intense over the past five years. Other coaches started seeing our success and they wanted a piece of the action. However, I'm still happy with the audiences we are attracting and the lives we are changing for the better through our Summit event.

SIX BIG STEPS FOR GROWTH

People ask me all the time, "How did you get so many people to come to your event?" I want to share with you the six key steps that I used to grow the Summit into the largest business conference for the childcare industry as well as a multi-million-dollar event. Whether you want to create a huge audience or just have a moderate consistent following, you can use this formula to build your event, do successful launches, or grow a brand:

Step #1: Create Something UNIQUE That Your Niche is Starving For

Here's another famous Dan Kennedy saying: there's riches in niches. You want to niche your event as tightly as possible. For example, don't just target female business owners. Target female business owners who are making between $500K-$1 million a year and helping clients with executive services. If you do it right, your target attendee will have a "this is for ME!" response when they see your offer.

Then, you want to study ALL the conferences that are currently being offered for that attendee in your chosen niche. Make a spreadsheet or a grid and write down as many features and benefits of those competing conferences as you can find. Study their pricing and what's included in a ticket. Then craft something **truly different and unique** from everything else that's out there. Dare to be a little crazy. Get people talking about you. Tell your fear to be quiet and go ALL IN.

Step #2: Market Early and Often

We generally follow the same promotional schedule each year because it works. We actually start marketing next year's Summit at the one prior. Attendees of the 2021 Summit got a "down and dirty" ticket offer if they registered and paid for the 2022 show one whole year in advance. Usually, 60-70 people would take us up on it. So that was a nice base of attendees to work from, and it got us about $20,000 in revenue which helped cover future marketing costs. We then offer a Super Early Bird deal about 7 months prior to the event, then an Early Bird, then a Summer Deal, and so forth. For each promotional period, we would heavily market the deadline of that special price and that offer. Nearly half of sales would happen on the *day of* the deadline, which just proves that "FOMO" marketing really does get people to buy.

Step #3: Create Sizzle with the Steak

Your marketing offers, copy, and images all need to be exciting. They've got to sizzle and get people amped up. If the nuts and bolts of your offer is strong but boring, it's not going to sell. Another Dan Kennedy mantra: the #1 marketing sin is BEING BORING. Here are some questions to ask yourself as you finalize your event website and ads:

- ► Is there an attention-grabbing headline that pulls the reader in?
- ► Is my offer truly *irresistible*? So good that people can't pass it up?
- ► Are the images showing people's faces smiling and having fun? Maybe dancing or getting a photo with a celebrity speaker?
- ► Does the copy give me the "this is for ME!" reaction?
- ► Are there lots of reasons for people to want to be there?

If this is your first event and you don't have any real photos from prior shows, use stock photos that feature people who look like your target clients. Get sizzle reels of video footage from your speakers. Most speakers have these ready to go. Compile a video of what people are saying about you plus "sexy" shots of the city and venue, the hotel amenities—even the food and cocktails you're serving. Make it fun!

Step #4: Feature Lots of Social Proof

There are software apps that automatically collect video and written reviews for you and feature a "widget" you can put on your website, so it's all done for you. The one I use is called SoTellUs. Another popular one is TrustPilot. My SoTellUs widget on the Summit website features over 500 testimonials from attendees, many of them in video format. It's an incredible amount of social proof shown to anyone who is thinking about registering. My target client can see hundreds of people from their industry saying great things about the conference. This helps the show pretty much sell itself!

Step #5: Use Partners and Celebrity Speakers to Help You Fill It

We've got a handful of strategic partners who are not only sponsors with a booth at our show, but we work together all year long to help each other grow through reciprocal referrals and joint promotions. It's in their best interest to help us promote the event, so more people come, and more possible buyers get in front of us. We give them a unique code or link to promote the event, so they can get credit for any of their clients who buy tickets. Or we give them super discounted "VIP" tickets to give to their best clients, which makes them look great and helps us out too. It's a win-win-win.

We have also spent money on celebrity speakers every year, which is a worthwhile investment. It creates great "buzz" for your event, when someone of the caliber of Daymond John (Shark Tank), Laila Ali (Muhammed's boxing star daughter), or Mia Farrow (well-known actress) speak on your main stage. Plus, they are often willing to do a promo video for the event and put it out on their social channels. This creates even more sizzle for the steak.

Step #6: Price It Right

Getting your ticket pricing right is really crucial. You don't want to leave money on the table, but you don't want to out-price your market. I had studied price with all my offers, and I knew anything around 500 bucks was a sweet spot. Anything closer to $1,000 was getting resistance.

We started the Super Early Bird at $597 for a buy one, get one ticket. That means you get to bring a colleague for free, and it makes those tickets very desirable. Super Early Bird was usually our top-selling ticket and sold to 100-200 people every year just during that two-week promotion. The best strategy here is to study your competition, and consider low-balling them if you can afford it, just to gain audience. So, if they charge $800 a ticket, test an offer for $697.

MEETING DAYMOND JOHN

My favorite celebrity speaker of all the greats we've had is Daymond John, star of the hit TV show *Shark Tank*. When I met Daymond for the first time backstage, he was different than almost all the other celebrities I've met. What set him apart? He was truly interested in who was in the audience, and he wanted to know MY story. He was authentically trying to connect with me and understand what made this event tick. He's a great listener and very present. In my experience, most other celebrities are self-absorbed and full of ego. They don't show much interest in others. Daymond was different.

After Daymond did his keynote talk, he wanted to hang out. He's the only celebrity speaker I've ever hired who spent time walking around the exhibit hall with me, doing an impromptu meet-and-greet with all the sponsors. He truly lives and breathes entrepreneurship. He wants to understand the trends and "what's hot" in every part of business. This makes him a great businessperson, and this is why he's incredibly successful. He knows it's not about him—it's about the customer.

I told Daymond that my son Owen was a HUGE *Shark Tank* fan because as a family we watched the show with our kids, and then Owen continued to watch re-runs and new episodes of the show as an adult. Devin and I raised our kids to think like entrepreneurs. We wanted them to understand core principles of business, whether they ever started their own company or not. When Daymond heard this, he was super jazzed. He said, "Where's your son now?" I said, "He's a diesel mechanic in Wyoming."

Daymond then asked to see my phone. He went to the Photos app and clicked the video setting. He made Owen a personalized video on my phone. He's like, "Hey, Owen, where you at, man? You should be with us here in Orlando, but I heard you're doing great things in Wyoming! Maybe you could come join me on *Shark Tank* and be the next Shark!" I was absolutely over the moon that a man of his caliber would take the time to make my son a video. When I sent the video to Owen, he texted back, "Whoever said don't meet your heroes was wrong." This obviously made a wonderful and important impact. Thank you, Daymond! What an outstanding guy.

SELL YOUR ASS OFF

If you are committed to growing your business, there's going to come a time when you have to look in the mirror and make the shift. You have got to be willing to sell your ass off. And you've got to inspire your team, especially your sales or enrollment team members, to sell their asses off too.

I've hired some great salespeople in my time, and they helped us grow the Academy coaching program to over 200 members by 2020. And by 2023, we'd hit 300 members. This was the rocket fuel for the company's growth. In fact, it helped us achieve one of my biggest career goals—INC Magazine's Top 5000 List of Fastest Growing Companies in America.

I vividly recall the day I got the email from INC Magazine that we had made the list. It was August 7, 2020. I was sitting in my home office when all of a sudden BAM! We did it! We came in at position 3,764 of the 5,000 companies on the list. Other than that first online order that made me grab the champagne back in 2009, this was probably the best email I've ever gotten related to the business. After that, we didn't look back. We are one of the very few companies in the world to have received the honor not once but FOUR years in a row, consecutively, from 2020 through 2023.

Many small business owners I've coached have faced resistance or reluctance within themselves to embrace SELLING. I teach them that "sales is service." I want them to shift their mindset about sales and think of it as being of service to potential clients who desperately need what they have to offer. In this case, it's parents who are fearful or uncertain about what daycare program is right for their child. It's a tough decision to put your 12-week-old infant into care and to be able to TRUST that the child will be safe and protected. So, shifting your sales process to intentionally building trust with prospective clients might be the lever that swings doors wide open for your business. Regardless, you've got to be proud of what you offer and be of service to your customers, by embracing sales and marketing— no matter how scared you are. Because honestly, you are doing your clients a *dis-service* if you don't close the sale, or if you stop short of making the offer. People love to buy stuff; you just need to show them that you're a great fit to resolve the pain they are experiencing or to gain the benefit they want to have. Sales is yet another way for you to authentically find your voice and share your vision with the world.

When you speak your truth, you feel your heart and your head come together. The first step is to feel your truth fully in your heart, and to know from an intuitional place that it's right and real. As a leader, sometimes the truth might not be popular and might require hard conversations with your team. It may be helpful for you to reframe "difficult conversations" and call them growth conversations or coaching moments instead.

Finding your voice can help you gain confidence and over time, you become a stronger leader and CEO. It can also make you a better spouse, partner, or parent.

By the end of 2019, I felt really at home in Carbondale. Things were going well with my romantic relationship, and the kids were doing well in the Roaring Fork schools. I loved hosting my podcast and the company had about 20 employees at this point, so I was able to keep delegating things not in my Unique Brilliance quadrant. The growth of the company reflected the good energy that I was bringing as its leader.

I was excited for the new decade and my son's graduation in the spring of 2020. The kids and I celebrated the coming year by spending a few days with my mom and stepdad in Sarasota, Florida, during the Christmas-New Year's break. It was great to spend time with the grandparents as we approached my son's last semester in high school. Like all of us, I could never have anticipated what 2020 would bring.

◀ EXERCISE ▶
Antidote to Fear #6: Speak Your Truth

What does it mean to you to "speak your truth"?

When is a time you spoke your truth even though it may not have been popular or well-received?

In the above scenario, how did *speaking your truth* make you feel? (*Check all that apply*)

☐ It made me feel more confident

☐ It made me feel more powerful

☐ It clarified my purpose

☐ It aligned me with a core truth

☐ Other: _____

How do you feel about selling? Can you see that "sales is service" for the right client or customer?

_____

_____

_____

_____

_____

_____

_____

_____

_____

_____

"Do not anticipate trouble, or worry about what may never happen. Keep in the sunlight."

BENJAMIN FRANKLIN

"You either win...or learn. There is no such thing as fail."

KRIS MURRAY

CHAPTER SEVEN

SHARE YOUR WINS

E ver since my ex-husband left the business in 2015, there was a gap of opportunity in my company that I was keenly aware of, but I didn't know how to harness. There was a clear need for done-for-them services for the clients who had dollars to spend but didn't want to do it *themselves*. Specifically, clients wanted us to create beautiful state of the art websites that were also keyword-rich and could gain market share on Google. In addition, they wanted help with social media and digital advertising. These were all things we taught them *how to do themselves* inside the Child Care Success Academy (CCSA), but a large group of higher end clients just wanted us to do it FOR them.

I knew I was leaving seven figures of income on the table. I just didn't know how to build these services for clients without completely exhausting myself. I simply did not have the bandwidth to create a digital marketing agency and hire a top-talent marketing team on top of all the other stuff in my life I was handling.

THE BIRTH OF "GROW YOUR CENTER"

Enter Bruce Spurr. When I met Bruce in 2017, we were in a private Facebook group together for online marketers. It was a Frank Kern mastermind group—the same guy I got the $1 book promotion idea from. I saw Bruce on the Facebook group chat talking about some cool digital marketing concepts and he sounded very smart. (I was not wrong, as I later found out Bruce is an actual rocket scientist, so yeah, he's a smarty pants LOL). He and I got to chatting and connected right away.

I soon hired him as a consultant to run the digital marketing campaigns for my company. Then we started to talk about the opportunity that existed to blow things out of the water and help the Academy clients, now at about 225 potential clients. I invited Bruce to one of our quarterly mastermind retreats to do a session. He decided to start his own enterprise on the back of that first session when he got 35-40 clients to immediately raise their hands to work with him.

He and I could clearly see after that "market test" that there was a pent-up demand for digital marketing services among the CCSA clients. We just had to go after it. So, in August of 2018, we formed a partnership LLC called Grow Your Center. We were off to the races. We launched Grow Your Center (GYC) as a "sister company" of CCSA to the marketplace via the podcast and a big splash to the existing clients.

Those first couple of years were a wild ride—and wildly successful. We got to our first million bucks in revenue really quickly and then grew exponentially. The companies were well integrated as Bruce was on the leadership team of Child Care Success. Likewise, I helped in all the main leadership decisions of GYC and in the copy decisions for the websites. Copywriting has always been one of my strengths, and the team leaned on me to make sure the copy was as strong as possible in terms of marketing the unique benefits and features of each preschool client.

Grow Your Center quickly became the leading digital marketing agency serving the childcare industry exclusively. I felt happy and excited that I found Bruce and we were working together well as partners. It was a great strategy to add another company to my portfolio and expertise, but having Bruce mainly run the show protected my energy so I could still focus on growing the core business.

LEADERSHIP LESSONS

I always say, leadership is not for the faint of heart. Leading a large team was my number one focus at this point. There have been so many books written about leadership, and I was reading tons of them throughout this time, trying to get better. I studied under people like John Maxwell and Simon Sinek so I could learn what to do and what *not* to do when it came to managing people.

I particularly loved the book *What Got You Here Won't Get You There* by top executive coach Marshall Goldsmith. I was inspired to invite Marshall to speak at the 2021 Summit in Vegas, and he accepted. Marshall was just the loveliest human to hang out with. He is SO humble and joyful, as well as wisely brilliant. I also had him as a guest on my podcast, one of my all-time favorite professional experiences. In that episode, Marshall shared the three top characteristics of a good leader: courage, humility, and discipline.

I had made plenty of screw-ups as a leader. From Marshall and from my own experiences, I learned that humility was an important aspect of leadership for me to lean into. One of my top mistakes was making what I felt were innocent comments about a situation, only to discover that I had either offended a team member or made them feel bad. Yikes. It seemed like as the team grew, I was having to look in the mirror A LOT to really be honest with myself and learn from my mistakes.

One big lesson that I learned was around hiring and firing. I became aware of the leadership mantra "hire slow, fire fast" through one of the peer groups I was in. I think this might be the hardest part of being a leader or manager—hiring the RIGHT person and taking your time to do so (Hire Slow) and then letting go of someone who's not a fit or who's toxic in your organization as quickly as possible (Fire Fast).

There's an art and a science to hiring. You can use assessment tools like StrengthsFinder, DISC, or the Predictive Index to help you learn more about the candidate's professional "DNA." These tests allow you to compare the natural strengths of candidates to one another and hopefully discover who's going to be the best fit for the role. But there are hidden nuances to hiring that can make it really challenging, and if you've been in the leadership seat you know how tricky it can be. For example, how emotionally intelligent is that person on the inside? What are his or her emotional triggers and how does that fit with the rest of the team? The emotional stability of your candidates is not really something you can glean through the interview process. Of course, you can get clues by asking the right questions and giving them some workplace auditions or projects to complete onsite.

Perhaps the area where I struggled most is when it came to hiring the right COO or "captain number two" to work alongside me as CEO. I found it was hard to get the right mix of strengths for someone who was going to be the Operations Chief of Staff. They needed to understand metrics and be data-driven to make sure the company was hitting its goals. They needed to be good with processes and structure to optimize operations and drive efficiency. But they also needed to be good with *people* and be a solid leader to inspire the leadership team and all employees to do their best work and love what they do. As a result, we had some heavy turnover in that position from 2021 through 2023, and it was a tough time for me to keep everyone's morale high. After our second COO was let go after less than two years, I opted to do both the CEO and COO roles myself. I didn't want to make a bad decision again.

Throughout that time, I just kept pouring motivation and goal-oriented leadership into my team. The vision was clear about where I wanted us to go. I just needed to keep them focused and energized to get there. I'll share the importance of having a clear vision (and making sure everyone on the team KNOWS your vision) later in the book.

GAINING TRACTION

A few years prior, my brother Rob had given me a book off his library shelf when I was back home in Ohio for a visit. He handed it to me and said, "This book changed my life. Read it and then go do what it says."

You'll recall, Rob was the brother I worked with at the bolt factory in Cleveland. It was about eight years at this point since I'd left. During that time, Rob had grown Auto Bolt into a very successful manufacturing company, using as his primary tool, the book *Traction* and the EOS Methodology (Entrepreneurial Operating System). This was the book he was now handing me.

I said, "Well, your business is obviously doing great. Thanks. I'll take it home and read it."

I didn't finish it. I read the first few pages, and it was quite frankly hard for me to get into. I put it on the shelf and forgot about it.

A year or so later, I saw Rob again. He said, "Did you read *Traction* yet?"

Sheepishly, I admitted that I had not. He offered another avenue: "Just go check out EOS Worldwide online. Hire yourself an EOS Implementor, and they'll show you how to get started. If you don't like it, there's no obligation to keep going with it. And here's a video on YouTube to watch to tell you what it's all about."

To me, that seemed like a much better way forward. I learned from the video that EOS is a model with six key components for how to run a small business. Any business with revenue of $2-$20 million could use it. The six key components are:

- ▶ Vision
- ▶ People

- ► Data
- ► Issues
- ► Process
- ► Traction

I hired an EOS implementor, based in Denver, to help us get started. His name was Stuart Robertson. Stuart first came in and showed us how to run an L-10 weekly meeting with our leadership team. L-10 is short for "Level 10". That means on a scale of 1 to 10, with 10 being the best, your meeting is ideally a 10 out of 10. Each week, at the end of the meeting, every person who attended rates it on that 1 to 10 scale. This gives everyone a voice and puts them on equal footing.

After that first experience with Stuart running our meeting and showing us the meeting flow and structure, we were hooked. We started using the EOS Model to run our company. And yes, I started using the book *Traction* as a detailed how-to manual with all sorts of tools inside it. Gino Wickman, the EOS founder, has written several great books related to business. *Rocket Fuel* is an excellent book, helping CEOs understand the visionary role and how to hire and utilize a great "integrator" for your business. More about this in the next chapter.

We discovered that our company was strong in several of the key components, like Vision and People. We had a strong culture. But in the areas of Data and Process, we were weak. We didn't have a consistent set of metrics to run the company by, which EOS called a scorecard. And we didn't have a written set of Core Processes, let alone a full Operations Playbook. So, we started working on those areas. It was a lot to take on. But the leaders and I could see that it was going to provide us with much-needed structure and foundation to take the company to the next level. And it's a good thing we did, because we had no idea what we were going to face in 2020.

A COVID-STRICKEN WORLD

Where were you when you first heard the word "coronavirus?" What happened to your world in March 2020? I bet you had the wind knocked out of your sails in some form or fashion. You may have even lost loved ones to the virus.

I felt like a ship at sea with no compass and very few lifeboats.

My kids and I were in disbelief at first. We thought the world *must* be overreacting. I remember saying "this will be over in six weeks." How I wish I had been remotely close to accurate.

My daughter had been training for months to compete in her first multi-state dance competition that spring. CANCELLED. My son had Senior Prom that April. CANCELLED.

Trips, business events, fun outings, book club with friends. ALL CANCELLED. My son was set to graduate from high school in May 2020. This of course could not be outright cancelled. But we had it outside in the parking lot. Everyone hung out on the back of their pickup trucks or in cars. One cool aspect was a drive-by parade that we had afterwards, where everyone in town came out of their homes and businesses to congratulate the graduates and wave us along.

My leadership team and I went into major pivot mode. First and foremost, we focused on our clients' needs and fears, and worked 24-7 to develop tools and strategies to keep these child-care centers ALIVE and in business. We called each and every client and had long tearful conversations with many. We were their shoulder to cry and lean on. Many of them were told to pause operations entirely by their state government, while others were able to operate almost business as usual. It was a huge variation in experience, based on state or even county. Trying to keep track of it all was impossible—and exhausting.

Our team of coaches dove in double-time to help all their clients and I was so proud of them. As the founder and CEO, I had a LOT of tough decisions to make in 2020. Of course, we knew that the remainder of our planned conference events had to be shifted to virtual (via Zoom) rather than in person. Luckily, we were able to get out of our high-priced hotel contracts due to the "Force Majeure" clause which keeps the client protected in case of events out of one's control, like natural disasters or crazy worldwide viruses.

There was so much FEAR in the world. I had to keep my own fears at bay, and it required a consistent mindset practice. But I could feel that this was my time to lead people out of fear and help them remember that they were bigger and more powerful than they realized. People seemed to respond to me in a new way during and after COVID. They could feel my truth, my heart-felt desire to really help. I think they could tell it was genuine and authentic.

That October we pulled off the first (and only, so far) *virtual* Child Care Success Summit. We had over 1,100 people on Zoom with us for three days. People were intensely looking for connection—and survival strategies. It was surreal. Another top moment of my career took place when I got to interview the great Simon Sinek as a "main stage" Q&A speaker. I did one of the best pitches ever from a virtual stage, looking at over 1000 tiny cameras. And at the end of those three days, we had over 50 new clients say Yes to joining us in the Academy. It was exhilarating to connect with so many people during such a crazy and challenging time in our history. And also, I was tired. My daughter and I went home from LA and rested for a few days after that.

WHAT'S NEW & GOOD?

When I was in Fabienne Frederickson's coaching group back in 2012, she had us do an exercise called "What's New and Good."

It's basically a win-sharing exercise, designed to get business owners to focus on the GOOD stuff they've accomplished. It's so easy when you're running a company to focus on all the bad news. The people you had to fire or angry clients you had to deal with. Maybe a lawsuit, or the plumbing system that had to be replaced. Right?? This practice of writing down, sharing, and celebrating our wins every quarter totally boosted my confidence as a young entrepreneur. It was probably the biggest game-changer and energy-shifter I did every three months like clockwork.

In fact, you can do this practice every week or even every DAY to really power it up. There's an app you can put on your phone called Wins Tracker. Talk about a way to stay focused on your accomplishments! If you celebrate three wins every day, big or small, that would add up to a whopping 1,095 wins for the year!

Fabienne and her husband Derek also shared that they regularly did this practice with their children at dinner time. Over the evening meal, they'd say, "Hey, kids! What was new and good today?" Each would take a turn sharing, and they said every member of the family felt happier and more confident when those wins were shared, even by the youngest member of the family.

I modeled this too. With clients we've done it at EVERY quarterly member retreat since inception of the Academy. With my kids, it was a common dinnertime practice. And it was awesome. Sharing wins is one of the BEST ways to overcome fear and create more confidence within yourself and your teammates or family members.

Over the years, we have intentionally *evolved and improved* the experience for Academy members at our live mastermind retreats. Like I said all the way back in Chapter Two, it's all about VALUE. I was always looking at how to make the member experience better. More fun. More impactful. More irresistible, so members would stay plugged in longer.

The list for what we did to uplevel the programs is LONG, and I don't want to bore you. One of the coolest things we've done is create meaningful client appreciation and award programs. We want people to feel special. The movers and shakers in the Academy get rewarded and SEEN. They get big shout-outs. They also get CASH. This motivates folks to share their wins even more. The Child Care Rockstar annual winner gets $5,000 cash, plus an all-expenses paid VIP trip to spend a private coaching day and fancy dinner with me. We also celebrate the Owner & Director of the Year and have created new awards like Rising Rockstar and Trailblazer. These go-getters receive beautiful, monogrammed awards they can display in their offices. We know that sharing wins is such a powerful practice, we've made it nearly impossible for people NOT to.

TURNING FINANCIAL NIGHTMARES INTO WINS

I want to end this chapter by sharing with you another big WIN that I accomplished during this time—and it's a personal one. Back in 2008, during the "great recession," Devin and I owned five rental properties. These properties were all located in and around the Cleveland, Ohio area. The economics of these single-family homes were not good. We were struggling with keeping them rented with good tenants and maintaining a positive cashflow. In one of the units, we had to wait months before we could evict a non-paying tenant, only to find a huge hole in the ceiling that was causing damage to the rest of the home. And that was BEFORE the recession.

We made the sad but necessary financial decision to let them all go back to the bank. We simply stopped paying the mortgages, and the banks foreclosed on us. We avoided bankruptcy, but we had terrible credit and a seven-year wait until these black marks on our personal finances would flow out of our credit file. I was ashamed and embarrassed. My family had questioned our decision to get into the single-family home market in the first place, and now it felt like we proved them right. It looked like we had made foolish decisions, when we were only trying to get financially ahead in real estate. Our hero in this sector was Robert Kiyosaki, author of *Rich Dad, Poor Dad*. We believed in buying real estate assets, and I still do to this day. But at that time, the situation was bleak. How was I going to grow my newly founded coaching business into a success with no cash and just one low-balance credit card?

The foreclosures didn't fully hit my credit report until the spring of 2013, so I technically had to wait until the spring of 2020 to get free of my embarrassing history. I quietly asked clients and friends if they had any trusted resources that could help with credit repair. I got a recommendation from a San Diego client to get in touch with Bill Ipsan of Ipsan West. I am very grateful to Bill (and Arianne, who referred him) for helping me with my file. Within about nine months, my credit was fixed. I had to pay off some old debts to get the foreclosures settled and removed from my file. But it was SO worth it. Since that time, my FICO score has gradually increased and now it's hovering around 820.

This was a HUGE win for my life. I could now get a loan to buy my dream house! I could get business credit, including an American Express Platinum card—one of the best cards out there for rewards and points, especially if you travel.

Yes, I may have had moments of self-doubt and fear about my money situation. But I never let my bad credit score stop my positive mindset—or stop me from growing the company. I always believed things would work out, and that money would show up when I needed it to. Sharing my wins kept me confident and out of fear mode.

◄ EXERCISE ►
Antidote to Fear #7: Share Your Wins

Do you have a regular practice of sharing your wins with yourself, your family, or your work colleagues? If not, how could you start one?

_____

_____

_____

_____

_____

_____

_____

_____

_____

_____

_____

How does **sharing your wins** make you feel? (*Check all that apply*)

- ☐ I feel more confident
- ☐ I feel more courageous to face the next challenge
- ☐ It makes me feel gratitude and appreciation
- ☐ It helps me remember everything I've accomplished
- ☐ It helps me have a positive mindset

How can you help other people in your life share their wins more often?

"*If you are working on something exciting that you really care about, you don't have to pushed. The vision pulls you.*"

STEVE JOBS

CHAPTER EIGHT

HOLD YOUR VISION

A s you build your business, it's important to keep the exit in mind. What's your exit strategy? At what age and what wealth number would it meet your goals to exit? Get really clear about what your end game is. I had been pondering and thinking about this for the past few years.

In one of my mastermind groups, I learned about something called an ESOP: Employee Stock Ownership Plan. Turns out, my business and my situation were a great fit to use an ESOP for multiple reasons. First, it would convert my S-Corporation structure into a tax-free entity. The company would owe *zero tax* to Uncle Sam or to the state of registry. This is because of laws passed by Congress back in 1986 and again in 1996 (the Small Business Protection Act), allowing any S-Corp that was employee-owned to pay no tax. This was an incredible discovery for me! Because at this point with our company generating around $5 million in revenue each year, taxes were a huge expense and burden.

We could take the tax savings and invest it in growth or save it for our nest egg. This was a massive cashflow strategy.

The second reason to do the ESOP was personal. It would allow me to sell the company to my employees and exit from the business. The typical time frame for this is five to six years after becoming an ESOP. I was then 52 years old. This would enable me to exit before the age of 60, which was my goal. I had been feeling kind of tired of being the CEO lately. I had decision fatigue. I needed a new path and a new vision for my life. I didn't know yet what that would be, but a change was calling to me in my heart of hearts.

The third reason was that it was good for the employees. The people on my team had busted their butts to get us where we were. I wanted to leave a legacy and enable them to build wealth too. And I didn't want to sell my company to a private equity firm or a buyer whose motives were questionable. To be frank, I didn't want a buyer to come in and fuck it up. I wanted to protect the jobs and the vision for the team that was in place.

So, we got going with a group of ESOP attorneys to make it happen. Once the documents were all ready to be executed, the final important step was to get a third-party valuation firm to assess the company's value. It was valued at just shy of five million dollars. That was the amount that I exited for, and the payouts were scheduled. We didn't know how long it would take to pay off my note, but we set a goal to pay off about 15-20% of the note each year. Again, the goal was to fully exit by the time I was 58 years old. And I'd be a multi-millionaire.

Of course, in order to fully exit as both founder and CEO, I would have to find our next CEO to replace me. I didn't know then what that might look like, but I wasn't worried about it. I knew I had several years to groom someone from within or hire from outside the company.

2020 turned out to be an amazing year for me. The ESOP was done, I bought my dream home on the river, my son had graduated high school and was going to an automotive trade college, we survived COVID, and we had landed on the INC 5000 List. I virtually interviewed one of my heroes, Simon Sinek. We also took the kids on a dream vacation, spending 15 days whitewater-rafting on the Colorado River through the Grand Canyon. I felt like I had fulfilled so much of my original vision and expanded it to beyond where I thought possible. 2021 was just around the corner and we had eight coaches on the team now. I had truly created the dream business and life I always wanted.

DON'T EXIT TOO EARLY

I was really glad I had waited until 2020 to do the ESOP and now had a plan to exit in the mid seven-figures. Because just a few years earlier—back in 2017 when I was facing all those challenges like the employee lawsuit and the DUI—I almost threw in the towel. And when things get really hard, it's easy to want to sell the business and just quit.

It was October 2017, and the Chicago Summit event had just ended. After the event, I spent an evening with one of my besties who lives in a Chicago suburb, Jennifer. She and her husband Bram are two of my most trusted friends. They said, "Hey, come hang with us after your conference is done and we'll cook some great food on the grill and have a blast." I was there in a heartbeat. We got to chatting about business as we usually do. Bram has a great entrepreneurial mind. I was just exhausted and depleted from the event. As always, I had given it my all and had no energy left. I knew I would pop back to my normal self, but on this day, I was spent.

I was really feeling beaten down after the year I'd had. I said, "I got an offer to buy the company. And I'm thinking about accepting it."

Bram's head snapped back a little. He said, "What do you think the company is worth, and what's the offer?"

I said I didn't know, but I'd accept an offer in the ballpark of two million dollars. We talked about the annual revenue and net profit (EBITDA) of the company right now and what a valuation might come in at. Then he looked me straight in the eye and said, "Don't sell, Kris. It's too low. Hang on and keep building it. If you sell now, you'll regret it forever."

I felt the truth of his words in my heart and in my gut. I knew Bram was right. Even though I resisted the idea of continuing to push the boulder uphill, I dug my heels in and kept going. And I'm so glad I did. Because just a few years later, the company was valued at five million. And the ESOP was not only going to pay me that; it contained another component of wealth for the founder called "synthetic equity." I was going to be able to walk away with closer to $7-8 million total for my exit.

I tell this story so you can benefit from my near mistake. I almost sold for too little in a time when I *wasn't thinking clearly* because I was super depleted by my business and my life situation. I needed to weather the storm and come out on the other side, stronger. I needed to face my fears and know that they were just that—false experiences appearing real. I doubled down on myself and my business in 2018 and never looked back.

Later, after I did exit as CEO, I had dinner with Bram and Jen at one of my favorite restaurants—Gibson's steak house in downtown Chicago. He said, "Remember back in 2017, the advice I gave you?" I nodded with a big smile. I'll always be grateful for that clarity and the decision to back myself and trust the process.

A NEW CORPORATE OFFICE

My dream home on the river was great, and it had a home office, but I was feeling a vision for something bigger. I wanted a space where I could host clients and maybe even run small mastermind meetings. I was driving down a random side street in downtown Carbondale when I passed a cool-looking building with a "For Rent" sign in the window. It was a peach-colored adobe-style building surrounded by beautiful gardens, across the street from the town park. What a perfect spot for a corporate office, and my dog Simba would love it too.

I stopped the car. I immediately called the number on the sign. I just had a feeling.

The space was perfect. It had hardwood floors, a little kitchen, even a shower in the bathroom so I could go to my morning workouts then get showered and dressed in the office afterwards! Upstairs was a big open room with lots of windows that we would eventually turn into a mastermind meeting space, with 18 seats, conference tables, and a presentation wall. I was also getting into running online "challenges" on Facebook and Zoom, and I used this space for engaging groups of clients and prospects in front of my big whiteboard. It was awesome. It created an upleveled "look" to the world.

Every day that I walked into that office, it felt like home. It brought me so much joy. We covered the walls with canvas prints of client testimonials—social proof everywhere! This is a core idea we shared with clients too. Remind your team and your current clients of all the lives you've impacted by putting it on the walls of your business. You can never have too much social proof!

The office re-energized my passion for being the CEO and visionary of the business. I had needed something fresh, and this fit the bill. Besides, I was in the middle of home renovations that we were doing on the primary bedroom suite and then later, the kitchen-living-dining rooms. I couldn't work in peace and be on Zoom calls with clients with all that banging and renovation noise going on.

WHAT'S YOUR VISION?

Obviously, my vision for what the company could be had changed multiple times since it began in 2009. But I always had a clear vision. Sometimes it was based on revenue or number of clients served. Sometimes it was based on goals for my leadership team or overall employee structure. Along with the vision, we had core values that helped us create an intentional culture, based on a set of shared values.

I also created annual written "SMART" goals for myself both personally and professionally. This practice was one of the best things I did each year. By putting those goals on a sticky note or index card and posting it in front of me where I could look at it every day, nearly all of my goals were accomplished. It almost felt like a magical process.

You must have a clear, written vision for your company. Sometimes we teach it as a "Vivid Vision," which is a three-year vision for exactly what your company will look like and *feel* like three years from today. I got this idea and practice from COO coach Cameron Herold, another business friend that I met in a group called Genius Network. Cameron was also on my podcast sharing these concepts.

Not only do you need the vision to be crisp and clarified, you need to share it with everyone on your team, your stakeholders, even your customers. People will be ignited and inspired by your vision. You simply cannot over-communicate your vision. Similar to social proof stories, it's a critical pillar of your company's brand and value platform.

Visions change; I am living proof of that. Keep checking in with your vision as the years go by, and things evolve. The "vision conversation" is a built-in part of every annual EOS leadership meeting. Once a year, at least, you and your leaders should be checking in on the vision and values. Have they changed? Are they still relevant and on point?

One more key point here—it's absolutely normal for you to change your goals and you should give yourself permission to do so. It's important to pay attention to those "little whispers" that you feel land inside you. That's your intuition trying to guide you. If you believe in God, you might call it God's voice. It's an inner knowing.

When your goals and/or your vision simply do not align anymore—with either your business vision or who you are BECOMING—you need to shift. Sometimes growth is not a clean, linear process. The world is changing so fast, and largely because of technology, business is changing so fast. Give yourself grace that if you *feel* to change, make the change. Follow your FEELING. If ever you feel lost or unmoored, grasp the lifeline of your inner knowing. You may feel judged by people in your life for making these changes, or even quitting something you were once aligned with, but are no longer. Allowing your goals to evolve WITH you is a more powerful way to live. Not hitting a goal—or losing interest in it—does not mean you've failed. It means you've learned and grown.

Finally, make sure your vision is BIG enough. It should feel a little scary, even. It must be bigger than your available resources, so it pushes you to live outside your comfort zone. When you get it right, it enables your creativity, your flow, and your innovation. And when you're in the flow state, you don't feel fear. You're creatively building your company from a place of inner knowing and the present moment. You're able to hold your vision and carry it forward because you trust your process. Simply stated, *you back yourself*. Any people who are not a fit or who question your vision just flow out of your life, often without you having to *do* anything. If you stay focused on what you love, the people who aren't a part of that vision will naturally be re-gifted to the universe. This is the ultimate freedom in being an entrepreneur. And it's an incredibly fulfilling place to live.

COMPETITION KEEPS YOU SHARP

Over the past few years, it had seemed like coaches in general were multiplying like rabbits. In my chosen niche of childcare/preschool business coaching, things were no different. What once was a "blue ocean" of available clients, and very little competition, became increasing fierce. Players seemed to come out of the woodwork and now there were nearly ten active competing coaching organizations in the childcare space who were biting at our ankles and copying our stuff. They were even bold enough to take our client lists and send gifts to them to try to steal them away.

At first, I was extremely wary of competitors and protective of my "turf." I didn't trust anyone and guarded our intellectual property very closely. I had gotten burned a few years earlier by partners that I trusted who stabbed me in the back and stole clients. This happened a lot from 2016 to 2018, and then again in 2022.

Once again, one of my employees left the company and decided to compete with us dead-on. My coaches were all pissed off and so was I. We were more angry than fearful, but I found myself wondering why this pattern seemed to keep happening. I decided to let it go but after a few months, I realized that the increased competition was a good thing. Like anything that's challenging, it happened because it was SUPPORTIVE for me. I realized that we could continue innovating the services we delivered to clients and continue to make our company different, unique, and special. I stopped spending time and energy on what everyone else was doing and just focused on myself and my team. I stopped worrying about the "what ifs."

I was able to come to an even deeper level of peace with the competition because of someone I met in November 2021, and she changed my life. Her name was Kirra Sherman.

MEETING KIRRA

In fall 2021, I started to feel like I was in the wrong romantic relationship. Things were stagnant and I was feeling like I continued to grow and shine, yet my partner Charlie was stuck in his comfort zone. Ever since we had moved in together in July 2020, it felt like we were more roommates than lovers. It seemed like I was initiating everything in the relationship, from trips to dinners and date nights to intimacy. I was craving affection and connection. I felt like I was *invisible* a lot of the time and just moved through each day with very little passion. Of course, I kept hoping things would change back to the way we were before we moved in together, but as the months went by, I fell more and more out of love.

It was late October 2021, and the Summit conference had just taken place in Vegas a couple weeks prior. One notable part of the Summit was the Grow Your Center booth that my partner Bruce had orchestrated. It was just amazing—the theme was a Sea of Hearts. Bruce and the team had installed about six large neon hearts on floor stands all around the booth. They wanted to inspire prospects and clients that GYC is a heart-felt company and truly cares about them. We had their backs when it came to helping them grow and doing world-class digital marketing. That booth really made me proud to be the company co-founder.

On a call with Bruce after the Summit, I asked him, "Where the heck did you get the idea for doing the Sea of Hearts??"

He said, "I'm working with this mindset coach named Kirra. I was really stuck about what to do for the theme. She told me to close my eyes and take deep breaths. And what did I see with my eyes closed? A beautiful sea of hearts appeared. And we just went for it, based on my vision."

That vision was simply astounding. And I knew in that moment that I needed to meet this Kirra person. I told Bruce to make the connection. A few days later, I found myself on a Zoom call with her. It was right around my 55th birthday, November 6, 2021. I told Kirra that I needed her help with some possible big changes that I sensed were coming in my life, but I didn't know how to navigate them. We started our coaching calls together the very next week.

The path that Kirra took me on is a journey I remain on to this day. I'll share it with you much more in the following chapters. But suffice it to say, she helped me peel back the layers to realize my truth. In other words, she helped me process a lot of stuck emotions in my body that needed to be healed and released, so I could find my truth. Prior to meeting her, everything felt cloudy, and I was emotionally triggered A LOT. I was in my head more than in my heart. Kirra took me on a journey back to myself and it felt amazing. But also scary at times. And sometimes she could be really harsh with me to help shake me out of my self-protection habits. These were times when my ego stepped in or I was being "in judgment" of other people. I needed to find true acceptance of all the pain and judgment in my life and let it go, so it no longer had power over me.

By January, I had clarity about my love relationship. It was time to move on and walk a solo path for a while. Letting that go was painful, but it also felt very right. One of the most painful parts was telling the kids and breaking up the household. Charlie and I each had two children, and they were all teenagers at this point ranging from 16 to 19 years old. They were sad for us and for each other. We were a blended family for a season, and now that season was over.

The summer of 2022 rolled around, and I wanted to move out and get some space, taking my daughter with me. (My son Owen was in trade school in Wyoming at this point). My home was again being renovated, this time in the kitchen-living-dining areas. I thought about what I would love. And a clear vision—and then decision—showed up. I wanted to live in a cool apartment in downtown Carbondale near the office. I'd be able to ideally walk to work and live in an energized downtown area. That's how I felt I would spend my summer. I consciously held that vision of what I would love in my heart. And the most amazing thing happened: it manifested.

The charming two-bedroom Airbnb apartment literally connected to my corporate office space became available. The man that had it booked for the summer was ill and had to cancel his reservation. Earlier, I had asked my office landlord Mary for any local connections she knew about on my behalf, so she knew I was looking. When she called me up and said, "The apartment just became available, do you want it?", I was astounded and overjoyed. Yes!!!

I continued working with Kirra one-on-one for six months, and then I transitioned to her group coaching calls. The following year, I joined her mentor Amir Zoghi in his coaching group, and I attended two spiritual retreats—one led by Kirra in Mexico, and one led by Amir in Australia—that helped me take the work even deeper. More than anything else, this spiritual mindset path has changed my life and the vision for what my life could become.

Holding a clear vision in your mind and in your heart is a surefire way to quell any fears that rise up. When you use this strategy, you may find yourself manifesting something (or *someone*, as I'll share in Chapter 10) you would truly love. It can be a big thing for your life, or maybe a small "win" for your business. Regardless, remember to Hold Your Vision!

◄ EXERCISE ►
Antidote to Fear #8: Hold Your Vision

Do you have a clear vision for your business and / or your life for three years from today? If so, describe it in as much detail as possible. If not, spend time clarifying your vision and write it down.

_____

_____

_____

_____

_____

_____

_____

_____

_____

_____

_____

When is the last time you communicated your personal or professional vision to the following people?

- ☐ Spouse or significant other: _____
- ☐ Your children: _____
- ☐ Your employees or teammates: _____
- ☐ Your clients or customers: _____
- ☐ Your peer group or mentor: _____

How does holding your vision help you stay out of a fear-based mindset?

"*Our greatest challenge does not come from outside – it comes from our internal conditioned mind. Fear is produced by your thinking, not by the situation.*"

ECKHART TOLLE

CHAPTER NINE

SURRENDER AND LET GO

T he spiritual retreat that Kirra led in Puerto Vallarta was an intense week of surrender for me. I let go of so much emotional history during those seven days. I didn't realize how much stored emotion I was carrying around in my body. I shed old "stories" about family members, romantic relationships, and work situations. The biggest hurt that I let go of centered on my relationship with my dad.

When I was a kid, I knew my dad loved me and he was always there for me. But it was confusing. Because sometimes, he would say very hurtful things to me about my appearance. I know he was just trying to motivate me to be my best self physically. But he probably put too much importance on looks—especially my weight and my skin. I was a curvy teen, and I struggled with my weight. I had naturally large legs and rear end, and I was never going to be "skinny" unless I stopped eating and became obsessed about my weight in an unhealthy way. I also had a pretty bad case of teenage acne at that time. Needless to say, my self-esteem was on the razor's edge. Critical comments from my dad didn't help.

BECOMING A STRONGER LEADER THROUGH HEALING

As a result of that time in my life, I was still carrying deep emotions of low self-worth into my fifties. It was totally unconscious, but it affected my actions as a boss, a parent, and a lover. I placed expectations and agendas on the people in my life. I repeated my dad's negative behaviors by making little critical comments to my kids from time to time. I didn't love myself fully because I was still carrying these emotions. And that absolutely translated to how I was showing up in my life. At that Mexico retreat, I got these emotions out of my body by sharing them in our circle, writing about them in my journal, crying them out, and "leaving them at the gate." We had a gate at the top of the villa where we held the retreat and every time one of us needed to really release something big, Kirra would send us to the gate to surrender and let go.

Because of my past feelings of unworthiness, I had attracted people in my life repeatedly to bring the story of unworthiness back up again. This was actually supportive for me—even though in the moment it felt horrible—because it was helping me face the feelings. The pattern was shining a light on the fact that I had stored emotions of unworthiness. Once I processed these feelings and they left my body, the patterns of unworthiness STOPPED. It was healed. I had let it go—all of it.

One other story played out for me professionally as a business owner around this same theme. I hesitate to share it because it has healed, and I've let it go. But it was another place in my life where I had to face fear, and I used the antidote of *surrendering* to let it go.

I had an employee who played a big role in my company. Let's call him Bob. Bob was a great coach and ended up being a very successful salesperson for me. As valuable as his skills were, it always took a lot for me to manage him. Bob could be a bull in a China shop, if you know what I mean. He made comments that undermined me, and he said things that hurt people's feelings on the team. I got used to cleaning up his messes. It seemed like too much trouble for me to fire him, because he gave a lot of energy to the clients and he really helped me grow the company. But I always had a nagging feeling in my gut that he was saying and doing things behind my back that were not supportive. In fact, it caused me to question my self-worth as CEO. There it was again—this story of "unworthiness."

After three years of unnecessary drama and giving in to his frequent demands, I knew by the end of 2020 that things HAD to change. I had to part ways with Bob. We figured out a severance plan and a way forward that would allow both of us to "present a positive face" with the clients. Bob told me that because of his health concerns, he wanted to semi-retire, take time off, and just manage his rental properties. He said working so many hours had taken its toll on his health as well as his personal relationships. I wished him all the best and we entered the new year on a fresh path.

Bob had promised me he was absolutely NOT interested in doing any coaching with our clients. He said, "I never want to deal with any employees again." At any rate, he was on a one-year non-compete/non-solicit agreement after he left, so 2021 remained quiet.

You can imagine my shock when 2022 rolled around and Bob went against his word to not compete with me and my team. He created a coaching business with a mastermind group that directly competed with Child Care Success. We had three levels of coaching; he had three levels of coaching. Because he had worked with me on the inside for so long, he knew all our trade secrets. He went after us with a vengeance, and it felt very personal to both me and the coaches on my team who used to work with him.

I share this story because if you're an entrepreneur or thinking about starting your own business, there are going to be people that come into your world that challenge you. Whether they're employees, clients, mentors, or vendor-partners, you will likely feel an emotional charge or feel "triggered" from dealing with certain folks. If they're a key employee, you can protect yourself with policies like having them sign nondisclosure and non-solicit agreements when you hire them. Make sure they have a crystal-clear job description and that their behaviors fit your culture. If you see any toxic behaviors, manage them quickly OUT of the organization. If you can't right the ship, you need to let that person go as fast as you can.

But the biggest shift you may need to make, like I did, is **letting go of the story and the power that it has over you**. Process the emotions and sit in the discomfort. Talk about it with a coach or mentor, journal about it, sit with the emotions and cry it out. Do whatever it takes to surrender and let go. Find your way to *complete acceptance* of the actions of others who have caused you hurt over time. It can be a quick process or a very long one, but you don't need to rush. Personally, I left this story about Bob "at the gate" in Mexico so there's no longer an emotional charge for me regarding this issue. But I'm not gonna lie, it took quite some time to fully process it and let it go. Because it was hurtful, and that's okay.

Be gentle with yourself. Most importantly, don't ignore the emotions or push them down. If you do, they're only going to come back up later in another version of your story.

Here's the good news. From all the people I've hired and then had to part ways with, I've become a much stronger CEO and leader. It's also helped me be a better coach for my clients and teammates. And for all the love relationships I've had that ended, same thing. You grow and learn with each one. When you heal the past emotions and release them, your self-worth and self-love grows. **Your deservingness rises**. You trust yourself more deeply and you know you've got your own back. No one can ever take that away from you.

THE ULTIMATE LETTING GO

When I came home from the Mexico retreat, I felt joyfully neutral. So much emotional processing had left me feeling amazing, and like my "lifetime cup" that was holding all those old feelings was empty. I walked into my house on that day in early April 2023 after a long travel day very much looking forward to sleeping in my own bed. After giving hugs to my daughter and my dog, I unpacked a few things, brushed my teeth, and climbed into bed. Ahhhh.

An hour later, I still lay there unable to sleep. I was gripped with anxiety. All the responsibilities of my life came washing over me as I tossed and turned. My head ran amok with thoughts and worries—all the things in my business, my life, and my LONG to do list. My thoughts were driving me into overwhelm. I took deep breaths and tried to let go using the mantra I learned from my mentor Amir: "There's nowhere to be, nothing to do, nothing to accomplish, nothing to figure out." Eventually, my tired brain and body let go and I drifted into sleep.

On my next coaching call with Amir a couple of days later, I shared this anxiety-gripped experience with the group. I told them about coming home feeling so joyfully empty from the retreat, only to have all the worries and emotions come rushing into my body upon laying my head on the pillow.

Amir said point blank, "Kris, when are you going to get off the f-ing treadmill?"

His question stunned me. It's like he looked directly into my soul and called me out, to the very depths of truth. Zero bullshit. My fellow Inner Circle members waited with bated breath for my answer.

To be honest, I didn't know the answer.

My head was spinning. Since I had sold the company to my employees via the ESOP in 2020, I was taking financial payouts and thinking about shifting gears by leaving the CEO role. Honestly, I did feel like I was on a treadmill. I had been yearning to do something fresh and new, but I'd been the CEO of this company I founded for so long that I struggled with shedding this skin. My own identity was intertwined so deeply with the identity of CEO, I didn't know where one stopped and the other started.

But deep down, I felt the yearning. I felt the truth of that feeling, the inner knowing. COULD I step down this year? If so, when was the right time? Who would be my successor in the role?

I faced all these questions in that instant that Amir asked about the treadmill. My reply to him and the group was, "I'm not sure. Let me ponder on it and I promise I'll get back to you soon with what my heart wants."

That evening, I asked the universe (or God, I can't quite recall) to bring me the answer. When I opened my eyes the next morning, the answer was clear—November 1st, 2023—just six months away. I tried that date on for size in my soul, heart, and head. It felt perfect. Later that day, I set up a call with my chosen successor, Director of Coaching Jennifer Conner. As I've mentioned, Jen was the perfect choice. She had prior CEO experience of her own company, she was strategic as well as systems oriented, and she was my trusted friend.

I asked Jen, "How would you feel about becoming CEO on November 1st?"

She was excited and beaming. She gave a resounding "Yes!".

We communicated our decision to the leadership team, and they were all on board. Then in July, we notified the rest of the team in person with a champagne toast. We worked hard from the summer until November to get Jen and the team up to speed with all the little things in my brain that needed to be documented or systematized. The plan was, I would remain on the team as a strategic advisor to Jen, as well as continue my duties as podcast host, speaker/content creator, and Summit co-host. I would be working considerably less—just 5-10 hours a week. I was elated. This would enable me to free up my life so I could follow new passions and growth opportunities. I wasn't exactly clear yet what those were, but I wasn't concerned. Plus, I still had my role on the leadership team of Grow Your Center as a part-time CFO, which also required about 10 hours a week of my time.

ONE MILLION CHILDREN IMPACTED

At some point about eight to ten years after starting the company, we began to track our impact. Since impact was one of our core values, it made sense to figure out how many adults, leaders, educators, and children we were influencing with our leadership and business-building content and programs. In July 2023, we not only hit our goal of impacting one million children, we exceeded it! We ran the numbers and estimated that through the clients we had in coaching since the Academy was born in 2012, plus the books and online courses we sold, we had impacted 1.2 million children. Wow. We were happily stunned and shared the news with our members at our live retreat in Denver that summer.

We also went live on Facebook to share the news with the world and did a press release. Hitting this milestone meant so much to me and everyone on the team. I had just come back from a meaningful professional trip to New Zealand, where I had been invited to be the keynote speaker for a New Zealand childcare conference. We had over 400 owners in the audience, and I gave away a copy of one of my books to every person in the crowd. So I also felt the ripples of making an impact globally.

THE ANTIDOTE TO FEAR

EMBRACE THE VOID

Have you ever had a period in your life when you were just treading water? Or hanging out at home doing nothing and waiting for the phone to ring? After I stepped down from the CEO role, it felt so strange. It wasn't the same feeling as being home after losing your job, as it had no sadness, worry, or fear. It was just empty—swimming in a big void of nothingness. On November 1st, my first day of *not* being the CEO, I found my Star Seed Oracle deck of cards and just for fun pulled a card. It said "The Void." The card said to embrace the empty space where I was floating.

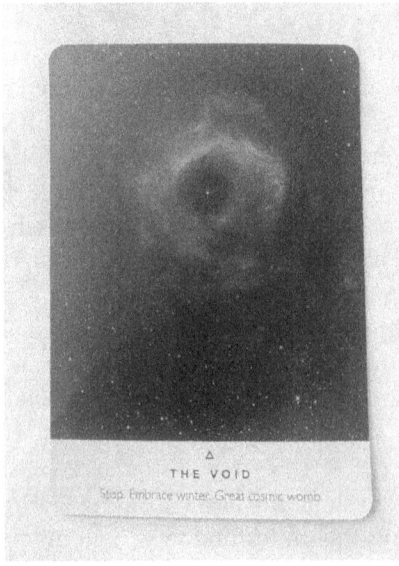

The Void tarot card

Where I found myself emotionally was a strange but beautiful mixture of calm peacefulness, kind of a blissed-out nothingness, blended with a little angst and nervous energy. I wanted to stay relevant and have a voice in the professional world. Yet, I wanted to travel the world and explore my bucket list.

TRAVEL, DREAMS, AND NEW LOVE

The first thing I did was lean into one of the items on my dream list, which was to go whale-watching in Hawaii during the month of February. I wanted to spend time really up close with the whales and dolphins, as well as my favorite animal, the sea turtle. I'd been to Hawaii before, mostly Maui, and felt a deep connection to the energy of the islands. But I'd never seen Kauai and never been to the north shore of Oahu nor the Hilo side of the Big Island. So, I made a plan. I would spend a full month in Hawaii, solo. Ten days on Kauai, ten days on the Big Island, and ten days on Oahu. I got online and found three great condos to rent, one on each island, for ten days each. Then I rented cool cars. Man, this was going to be an epic adventure! And I would finally get to see whales.

Another dream that I have is to visit all seven continents and at least fifty countries. I'd been to central America, but never South America. So, when I got invited by my friend Yanik Silver and his group Mavericks to be part of an impact trip to Ecuador, I jumped at the chance. The trip was co-led by Anita Sanchez, a native American author and speaker, and defender of indigenous peoples everywhere. My experience was super special, and I was happy to help support the tribal people that we stayed with and learned from.

A few people who went on that trip were also going to be at Burning Man, the "infamous" week-long festival that takes place north of Reno in the desert. These friends went every year and hosted a camp there. I had always wanted to experience Burning Man. Remember Camille, my first employee? Camille was the person who first introduced me to Burning Man and how much joy she got from that week in the dusty desert. The core principles of Burning Man really resonated with me, especially Radical Self-Reliance and Radical Self-Expression. I also loved the Gifting component. There is no money or currency of any kind at Burning Man. Just strangers giving to strangers. The art, music, food, fashion, and friendship were all incredible. It's kind of like "Mad Max meets Woodstock." Now that my kids were up and out of the house, I was able to finally experience Burning Man in August 2024 and check that off my bucket list. Another dream—fulfilled.

Over the past 15 years, I developed an important practice of dream-listing and goal-setting. Every year in the last week of December, I pondered and reflected. I made a list of the year's accomplishments compared to the goals I had at the beginning of that year. I wrote out what were wonderful surprises and what didn't go so well. Where I fell short of the mark, and what I learned from that part of the journey. I never beat myself up. I just took all that into account as I brainstormed with myself on goals and dreams for the coming year. This is one of the most powerful practices I still do and teach to others.

If you're not doing an intentional goal-setting practice, this can really help you get *really clear* on what you want in your life, and that allows you to manifest your dreams much more easily. I'll share more about how I manifest what I love in the next chapter.

In November of 2023, I had one more epiphany. I attended a New Moon Ceremony at a local yoga studio. The lady who hosted the ceremony taught us that the new moon phase is a wonderful time to plant "seeds" of what you want to show up in your life. In other words, it can be a great time for manifesting your dreams.

I had been dating on and off for the last year or so, and back in June I had gotten on a popular dating app called Bumble. But as I like to say, I had kissed a lot of frogs over those months. Living in a small town in the mountains of Colorado is not the best place to meet eligible bachelors in their fifties. It's full of non-committal ski bum dudes in their twenties and thirties. I wanted to "manifest" my true love, but it seemed like pickings were slim. I was trying to believe in the unlimited possibility and live in that open energy, but sometimes doubts would creep in.

Regardless, I was open to just staying single and loving myself as fully as possible. I was having fun with friends and not "being attached to getting attached."

Back to the New Moon ceremony, a girlfriend of mine shared with me that writing a love letter to your future partner *as if they were already in your life* was something she did that helped her meet her significant other. From what I could tell, there were two keys to making this work: first, come from a giving place, not an energy of "taking" or receiving. Focus on what you love to GIVE to a relationship. Second, act as if it's already here. It's done; it's *decided*. If you come from a place of lack and secretly fearing or believing that you don't deserve it, it will never show up.

The day after the New Moon ceremony, I felt ready and completely open. I lit a candle and a love letter poured out of me from a place of inner knowing and giving. It wasn't an "I want" letter. It was all about the joy, laughter, and love that was shared between this man and myself. It was about our love for being in nature together and exploring the best that life had to offer in ways that lit us both up. Even though I hadn't met him yet, I felt his presence alongside me and in my heart as I read the letter out loud and then blew out the candle. I felt it was manifested and I had no doubt it would show up.

On December 23rd, just about six weeks after the night I wrote that letter, I got a Bumble message from a man named Chris. It said "Hey, KK. Nice to connect." Shortly after that, we went on our first date. By our fourth date, I knew it was something special. One amazing thing about it was that he lived 20 minutes away in a neighboring town. So, we were able to really get close in a short period of time and not do a long-distance thing. A couple months in, we were already talking about getting married. As of writing this, we have been together over 18 months, and we recently got engaged! I'm so grateful to have this man in my life. Two things about him really stood out in that letter. I talked about his passion for life and his open-mindedness. And those traits are very present in my Chris.

BECOMING A TEACHER OF PRESENCE

After working with Kirra on this path of discovering my true self, I got re-acquainted with Eckhart Tolle, whose books I had read years earlier but somehow forgot their impact. I dove in again to *The Power of Now*, Eckhart's first book, listening to the audiobook version during car drives. Wow. His words landed in a new way for me. The meaning of "presence" was clarified for me, and I realized that so much of the fear I experienced was rooted in either past experiences or hopes for the future—but fear was not rooted in NOW. **There is no fear in this moment—** simply the joy of being.

I looked at Eckhart's website one day and clicked on Retreats. He and his partner Kim Eng were running a five-day retreat in Maui the following November! It was just after my 56th birthday. It had been 30 years since I'd been to Maui, and I had an incredible three weeks there in my twenties. I was so excited that I registered immediately for the retreat. During that Hawaii retreat, I experienced a new sense of presence and calmness. Being with several hundred souls who were on the same path felt very special. We did group exercises together and movement classes with Kim Eng. I was feeling my intuition strengthen. Or rather, my ability to follow the feeling was revealed. The noise in my head seemed quieter, which allowed me to dive into my truth more clearly.

At the end of that retreat, Eckhart offered a six-month intensive course called Teacher of Presence. It was for people who wanted to learn how to teach and coach others in the work. I thought about it but didn't join at that moment. After being home for a couple weeks, it became clear. I wanted to do the course. I signed up and dug in. The course began with an in-person retreat in Banff, Canada. My dad always had a fascination with Banff. It was supposed to be a place of intense beauty in the Canadian Rockies. Partly because of my dad, and partly because I was following my feeling, I booked my flight to Banff and said YES to the journey.

The Banff retreat was held at the famously beautiful Fairmont Chateau Lake Louise, which is one of the most scenic hotels in the world. Eckhart and Kim did daily sessions, and I went a little deeper on the topics of stillness, presence, holding space for others, and letting go of the story to reveal your true essence. I also became more aware of the two parts of every human: the being side versus the doing side. One cannot arrive at the essence of simply BEING by doing more and more do-ing. So many people, and especially women, are searching for self-worth tied to their to-do list and being productive. I started to allow myself to DO less, to just be still, and to find beauty in the nothingness.

Obviously, I was spending a lot of time, money, and energy on following this spiritual path. But why? Would it make me a better entrepreneur, coach, and leader? Would it make me a better parent and love partner?

The answer to those questions is a simple "yes." In being more present and less driven up and down the seesaw by my emotional reactions, I was better in so many ways. Yet, the real "why" for me was about my relationship with one person and one person only: myself. In small yet hugely meaningful ways, I felt myself coming back home to myself. To my truth. To the person I was becoming. I was becoming my next version.

◄ EXERCISE ►
Antidote to Fear #9: Surrender and Let Go

When is a time in your life that you had to surrender and let go?

_____

_____

_____

_____

_____

_____

_____

_____

_____

_____

_____

_____

_____

How did **letting go** of that situation, person, or struggle make you feel? (*Check all that apply*)

- ☐ I felt lighter and more spacious
- ☐ I felt more open and accepting
- ☐ I felt grateful to be able to let go
- ☐ I felt ready to move forward
- ☐ Other: _____

Ponder about situations of **surrender and letting go** that you may face in the future. What comes up for you?

"You can have anything that you want, as long as you don't want it."

AMIR ZOGHI

"This is your wake-up call to pay attention to your wake-up call."

KRIS MURRAY

CHAPTER TEN

BECOME YOUR NEXT VERSION

As my company was paying off my note for selling the business to the employees, it was a key wealth-building strategy for me to invest those funds in a variety of places. My favorite type of investment is real estate, because it's rooted in real assets (dirt and concrete) and it's relatively stable—generally more stable than the stock market. Real estate also gives great tax advantages through depreciation. I have several different kinds of real estate: fully passive multi-family properties (apartment buildings in Texas and Florida), Airbnb short term rentals, commercial real estate, and even a piece of a luxury hotel in Hawaii. I've learned a lot and enjoyed the ride—and most of these investments are slated to double my principal or even triple it. That means if I put $200K in, the target payout is $400K or higher over a five-to-seven-year hold period.

Obviously, I'm not an investment advisor, but if you want your income to support a wealth-building strategy—and I hope you do—you're paying attention to what's going on in the markets. Too many women (and a few guys) I meet have a "head in the sand" mentality when it comes to money. Investing and paying attention to your returns is a great way to feel empowered, and of course, the cash is the thing that will fuel your dream life.

Because I had some financial difficulties back in 2008-2010 (remember all those foreclosures and bad credit?), it was important for me to step into a powerful shift around money. I was working on becoming my next version spiritually, and I wanted my energy toward wealth to also be "limitless." So, I made some bold moves. I switched wealth advisors to a proactive team that my mom recommended. She said her returns had absolutely improved with this group of young go-getters, and they were really great to work with. They took the time to explain things simply and clearly, and the "why" behind their investment choices. I know making these kinds of changes can be scary and time-consuming. But it has really paid off. My returns are WAY better than they were with my old financial team.

TURTLE RIVER CONSULTING

My CPA advised me to create a new LLC for personal consulting and coaching, so I could run all my expenses through there and offset my personal taxes. He needed a name for the LLC. I thought, "What are my favorite things?" My favorite animal is the sea turtle. And I've always been a river girl, not to mention I have a gold-medal river flowing through my backyard. So, the name "Turtle River" seemed like a natural fit for my new company. In mid-2023, Turtle River Consulting LLC was born.

In November 2024, I launched a new business. It was centered on my passion for working with a new type of client—someone who was inspired by the transformation I've gone through in my business and my life, and who wants it for themselves. I call it "awakened leadership" or "spiritual mindset work" but in its truest form, it's a homecoming. It's a journey back to yourself, to the person you truly are and were meant to become. Because this work with Kirra and Amir has been the most life-changing path I've been on, I am super inspired to share it. I already had a base of clients and fans, so it made sense to launch a mentorship program to help people (mostly women) on this self-realization journey. I had owned my personal branded website, KrisMurray. com, for years. It sat dormant. So, I built the website to speak to this new client. I wanted just a few clients to start, because I was still working about 15 hours a week for both Grow Your Center and Child Care Success.

Today, about 10 months later, I've worked with six women business owners, one-on-one, on this path. I'm about to launch a group coaching program and my first spiritual retreat is set for February 2026 in Maui. This work feels like coming home, and it's so fulfilling. I'd like to share a few of the core concepts with you that have been game changers for me on this path.

RECLAIMING POWER

One of the best places I found to start—for myself and with clients—is to focus on a process called "reclaiming power." This concept centers on seeing where you may have power in other things or people outside yourself. Like me, it might be from something traumatic that happened in childhood that you never healed or came to terms with. It could be something quite painful or a repeating pattern in your life. This can cause you to over-give, be a people pleaser, avoid negative emotions, or hide from your truth. Any number of behaviors can show up because you've given your power away. It's totally normal to be afraid of sitting with the discomfort that's there or facing those old painful emotions. That's why getting the help of a coach in this area can be so useful.

My big story around this was around the core emotion of "unworthiness" and giving power to people who made me feel ashamed or who stabbed me in the back. Once I sat with the emotion and accepted fully that these situations happened to me to SUPPORT my healing, my power was reclaimed. I loved parts of myself that had been hidden or shoved down. I loved my shadow side. And it completely shifted how I showed up energetically. The story of my life became neutral in this area, and the pattern ceased altogether.

Reclaiming power is usually where we start because it helps you feel more deserving, and more spacious. As you clear out old emotional patterns, it makes space in the "cup" of your soul, heart, and mind. You are less tormented by all the noisy thoughts in your head because the mind gets quieter. It's a beautiful process.

CREATING SPACE – WHAT DO YOU LOVE?

You know how it feels to de-clutter your closet, organize your office, or throw stuff away in your over-crowded kitchen pantry? What about cleaning out your junk drawer? Whenever you make physical space—whether it's in your home, office, car, or human body—you are creating a larger container for openness and the ability to BREATHE. This is why everyone went nuts over Marie Kondo and her, "Does it bring you joy?" clarity method for de-cluttering. I often use a mantra I learned from Amir, when I need this kind of clarity: "What do I LOVE?" This is another way to tap into whether something gives me joy from a place of Oneness—or not. Is it something that deserves to stay in my sphere, or does it need to *go*?

When you create space, you're able to sense your intuition much more clearly. You can feel the inner knowing easier in your body and your mind. And you can "follow the feeling" with certainty. If your mind is super noisy right now, try a little de-cluttering wherever mess tends to pile up. Another great place to look is in your technology. If your Google or Outlook calendar is a mess, start there. Spending time organizing your schedule and cleaning up your inbox can be life-changing!

MANIFESTATION IS A GIVING PROCESS

I talked about this in the last chapter when I told the story of manifesting love in my life. When I wrote that love letter, it was from an energy of GIVING, not receiving. I had written in my journal the specific things I wanted to *give* to a new love relationship. It wasn't about how much money he makes and what he was going to *give me*. Here's what I wrote in my journal:

Question: How do I want to GIVE VALUE to a love relationship? How do I want to *light it up* for that person? How do I want to create something amazing for a new lover that is a giving process?

My answers:

- ▸ I want to simply be present for him
- ▸ I want to hold space for him when he needs space, and support him when he needs it
- ▸ I want to laugh hilariously with him to feel shared experiences of Joy
- ▸ I want to give pleasure and receive it fully
- ▸ I want to cherish the little moments together
- ▸ I want to live an extraordinary life together, but also a simply beautiful life

Lots of coaches that teach manifestation come from a more selfish energy. They focus on the receiving component. If you've tried to manifest your dreams and it hasn't happened, it's likely because you're not coming from an energy of *giving*. You might have envy, or think the Universe owes you something. OR you don't feel worthy deep down inside, to receive the thing you are trying to manifest. If you've got some stuck *unworthiness* energy, work on processing that first.

Over the past couple of years, my power in being able to manifest feels super-charged. This is because I am getting more and more neutral, more spacious in my body, and more able to follow the feeling. At will, I can take myself from a place of duality—or being in "two"—to a place of oneness. And when you tap into your infinite self, where you access the Divine, or God, or Source (whatever you want to call it)—when you manifest from a place of Oneness, it just shows up. It is decided. You've made a whole-hearted decision.

PONDERING

What does it mean to have a pondering practice? I learned about pondering from my spiritual mentors. Pondering is usually best done at sunrise, and it can also be good at sunset. It's also best done in nature. When you tap into the energy of a forest, a garden, a river, or the ocean, it can bring you closer to your natural state of limitlessness. It reminds you that you are not only a drop in the ocean, but the entire ocean in that drop. (Which is also a quote from the spiritual philosopher Rumi). Pondering is like meditating with your eyes open. You can use Amir's mantra I shared earlier to get you into a calm, neutral state: There's nowhere to be, nothing to do, nothing to accomplish, nothing to figure out. Breathe deeply and be the ocean. This might feel woo-woo, but I promise you if you actually go ponder on a regular basis, it can change your life. Because what comes in and lands for you will give you valuable and beautiful insights. You will feel like you're in the flow with all things. It will ignite your creativity and give you clarity for what you truly love. You will be able to follow your feelings more clearly and with less doubt or "head noise."

My desire to go to Hawaii for a month solo came from pondering. It just landed—go spend time with whales and have a beautiful adventure. I didn't fret about the cost or the logistics. I just booked it. When I came home from that month away, I felt like I had become a new version of myself. I felt changed somehow. I couldn't put my finger on it precisely, but the world looked a little different on my morning walks. I had gone deeper into the layers of my true self. Again, it might sound corny, but now that I've experienced living life this way, I love helping others on this path. It fulfills me to help them feel the shift, and they realize how light and joyful a regular day can be.

JUDGMENT AND ATTACHMENTS

Back in the day, I definitely didn't realize how many judgments I was placing on the people in my life, as well as strangers that I encountered in my everyday existence. From my kids or my employees to the guy who cut me off in traffic, I was being emotionally triggered and then placing judgments on those people because of the emotional reaction. This is the way many people go through life. They are jacked up and down on the seesaw of their judgments. This is what it looks like:

> I got a raise – this is GOOD!
> But... my new boss is a jerk – this is BAD. (This is a judgment)
> But... my boss likes me because I brown-nose him. GOOD! (Another judgment)
> But... now my co-workers don't like me. BAD.
> Well, who cares, I don't care about them anyways! They are all fakers! (Another judgment)

The person who is being driven by their judgments is letting *other people* or events cause the positives and negatives in their story. They are looking externally for validation, because their ego wants approval and acceptance from others. Remember how Ego looks for love in all the wrong places? Your judgments are keeping you in a false prison. When you remove your judgments, you find peace and freedom from what others think, and all the energy you are spending outside yourself becomes yours again to hold and cherish. You feel lighter because you're actually **laying down the energy—or bringing it back home—that you were spending on all those judgments**. Whew!

You realize that your true power—and the magic of your time on earth—is INSIDE you. It's not *external*. It's not in the daily events of your "story" or what Tolle calls your "life situation." Accept that the story is always going to go up and down. But as you come into accepting and loving yourself fully, those events lose

POWER over you. You can laugh at them and take life way less seriously. You come to truly accept others—even your children and spouse—for who they truly are. As Mel Robbins says in her amazing book, you "LET THEM." You accept, fully. And acceptance is the opposite of judgment.

As you walk this path, you realize that what's TRUE for you comes from within. It's an action, not a reaction. It does not come from a shiny diamond outside of you. It has NO AGENDA. It doesn't come from something you feel sorry for or have a judgment about. When you feel sorry for people, you are secretly judging them. That's a false form of empathy.

Attachments are a sister to judgments. The biggest attachments I used to carry were tied up in my expectations for a specific outcome. If I didn't get the outcome I wanted, I would get really disappointed and sometimes even throw a hissy fit. Can you relate? Because I was attached to life being a certain way. My self-worth was tied up in expectation. For example, I would think about a future trip that was planned with my loved ones and be SO excited about it for weeks and weeks. Inevitably, because I showed up with this frenetic energy of "this trip is gonna be SO AMAZING..." something would happen during the trip that disappointed me. My kids would act out or my spouse would have a huge temper tantrum, sometimes both. Then the whole week would start devolving into a shit show. If I had let go of the attachment for how the trip would go, none of this would have happened. Or if it did, I would have shifted into acceptance and seen it as "not a big deal." My love for myself is not tied to how the trip goes. My life has much deeper meaning, so the trip can't trigger me, no matter what happens.

Again, this is such a free way of living. I'm able to be fully "me" authentically, and I'm free of my triggers. Of course, little triggers occasionally surface that shine a light on where I can still do the work. But to use a dog metaphor, these triggers are little Chihuahuas, not Doberman.

WHAT'S PRESENT FOR ME NOW

Today my life represents a calm centeredness that feels neutral yet joyful. I've never been "more myself", more sure of my path, and more authentic. I'm constantly evolving into a new version as I go deeper on the journey.

As I write the final words of this book, I'm happy to share with you that my kids are doing great. My daughter Maeve is a junior in college at Savannah College of Art & Design (SCAD) and majoring in Fashion Marketing. She's spending the upcoming quarter abroad in France. My son Owen just moved to Alaska from Wyoming with his girlfriend Beverly. He's got a great job as a diesel mechanic in Fairbanks and basically wrote his ticket on the relocation. He and Bev are engaged. I'm watching my children become successful adults and that's the best payoff of anything in my life.

The original business—Child Care Success Company—is also doing fantastic. Jen Conner is a strong and systems-oriented CEO who is taking the business to new heights. I am still enjoying being its podcast host and co-host of the Child Care Success Summit conference. Grow Your Center is also thriving and growing with my co-founder Bruce Spurr at the helm.

My fiancé and I are planning to get married in front of a small group of family and close friends in June 2026. The ceremony will be in one of my favorite places on the planet, and where we got engaged—Crested Butte, Colorado. As you know, so many big moments of my life have happened there, and that's where this story really gained traction back in 2012.

Of course, I'm still making financial moves, investing in real estate, and building a new coaching business that can take me into my sixties with the joy I receive from seeing my clients have better lives and more abundant businesses. It's likely going to center on running retreats for female entrepreneurs where I can create a magical and transformational experience for them so they can see their possibility open up in front of them.

The core emotion I'm feeling these days is gratitude. Living in a space of deep appreciation and gratefulness, fear may show up for a second in my heart or my mind, but it usually dissolves quickly. And did you know, it's a scientific fact that fear and gratitude *cannot* co-exist? Becoming a lighter, more joyful version of yourself is the ultimate antidote to fear.

I wish you love and peace on your path.

◄ **EXERCISE** ►
Antidote to Fear #10: Become Your Next Version

What judgments do you find yourself making about others, and how might you release those judgments?

Where may you be attached to the outcome, or driven by expectations for someone or something to be a certain way?

If you committed to starting a pondering practice, what might that look like?

ACKNOWLEDGMENTS

I have deep appreciation for so many people. I'd like to take this opportunity to give thanks.

First and foremost, to my family. Thank you Dad and Mom, and my stepdad Dale, for all the support and examples you've given me over the years. Thanks to both sets of my grandparents, Bob and Kay Chapman, and Virginia and Cliff Kocian, for showing me so many flavors of entrepreneurship. To my brother Rob, I'm so grateful for the book Traction and all the good times we shared at Auto Bolt. Thanks to my children Owen and Maeve for the experience you've given me to be your mom.

To the incredible marketers and entrepreneurs who influenced me: Dan Sullivan, Frank Kern, Grant Cardone, Daymond John, Ryan Deiss, Perry Belcher, Joe Polish, Robert Kiyosaki, Gino Wickman, Keith Cunningham, Verne Harnish, Richard Branson, and the Cosmic Sloth himself, Mr. Yanik Silver.

To my mentors: Amir Zoghi, Kirra Sherman, Ali Brown, Fabienne Frederickson, Dan Cricks, John Maxwell, Bill Glazer, and most of all, Dan S. Kennedy. Dan, your Five Rings of Wealth for information marketers is pure gold. You gave me a proven blueprint to build this business, and for that I will forever be grateful.

To other incredible humans who have inspired me along the way: Scott Whitaker, Stuart Robertson, Julie Roy, Rachel Supalla, Darla LeDoux, Andre Norman, Stedman Graham, Glenn Morshower, Ann Rhoades, and the great Les Brown. Huge thanks to Marshall Goldsmith. Thanks to my two amazing fitness trainers who are also positive mindset coaches: Kyle Brown and Sandro Torres.

To my business partners Bruce Spurr and Jennifer Conner. You are both wicked smart, and you've made the journey really fun. I have deep appreciation for you both – more than I can express with words.

To my team, we could not have built this without you. The coaching team has morphed over time, and your contributions have all been incredible. To the coaches: Ben Poswalk, Tameenah Adams, Donna Jensen, Steve Lloyd, Jody Zabriskie, Chantel Pettengill, Tasha Santistevan, Ashley Varouhas, Kishani Woldberhan, and Jacob Jensen. Thanks to "Coach Jay" Jamarrion Tabor, and the always joyful Jennifer Slavin. To the operations and marketing teams, you are the backbone of the company. You keep us growing and doing great work. Special thanks to Braylen Eimer, Nina Zeddell, Tammy Lee England, and Carlo Canieso.

Thanks to my "other daughter" Camryn Conner for rocking my socials. Thanks to Blake Preston for being my accountability buddy when I wasn't in the mood to write.

To my trusted ECE colleagues and professional partners: Gigi Schweikert, Aleta Mechtel, Ron Clark, Gerry Pastor & Jane Porterfield, Bobby & Rick Franzo, Chuck Gibbs and the team at Line Leader, Jared Hall, The Sparkly One Samantha Phillips, and most especially, the incomparable Vernon Mason.

Thanks to Lil Barcaski and the team at GWN Publishing for lighting a fire under me to get this book written. I'm proud to say that no AI was used in the creation of this book.

To my clients and their leadership teams, who do some of the most incredible, difficult, and heartfelt work in this world. Thanks for helping us impact one million children plus, through your high quality programs and your education teams.

Finally, thank you to my partner Chris. You've kept me inspired, well fed, happy and loved during the journey of writing this book. I can't wait to marry you.

APPENDIX

Company Revenue History & Number of High-End Coaching Clients (Academy Mastermind)

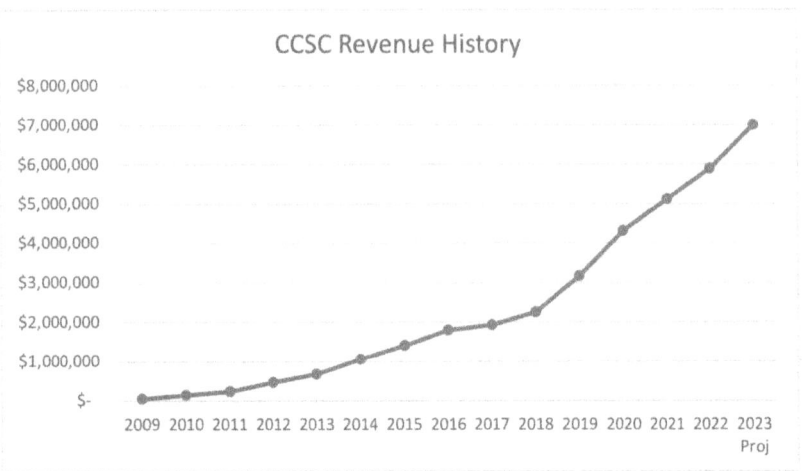

Company Metrics	January	Feb	Mar	1st Qtr Total / 3-Month Avg	April	May	June	2nd Qtr Total/ 3-Month Avg
Total Unique Visitors - Web	659	805	1413	959	1247	927	927	1034
Home page pageviews	604	856	1418	959	1324	1031	924	1093
Sales page pageviews	173	261	291	242	382	276	269	309
% of total	29%	30%	21%	25%	29%	27%	29%	28%
Total Opt-ins	89	113	182	128	222	136	113	157
Opt-in Rate	14%	14%	13%	13%	18%	15%	12%	15%
Confirmed Opt-ins step 1	45	70	88	68	88	119	113	107
% who Confirm	51%	62%	48%	53%	40%	88%	100%	68%
Free CD orders	18	23	33	25	38	23	19	27
Conversion from step 1	40%	33%	38%	37%	43%	19%	17%	25%
Amazing Free Gift orders			10		21	8	10	13
Conversion from Free CD			30%		55%	35%	53%	48%
Big kit sales (non-promotion)	2	1	1	1	2	1	3	2
Conversion % from sales page visitors	1.2%	0.4%	0.3%	0.4%	0.5%	0.4%	1.1%	0.6%
Adwords clicks	162	237	292	230	246	204	209	220
% of total uniques	25%	29%	21%	24%	20%	22%	23%	21%
Cost per Adwords Click	$ 0.36	$ 0.40	$ 0.41	$ 0.39	$ 0.44	$ 0.43	0.41	$ 0.43
Marketing Expenditure								
Adwords	$ 58.96	$ 94.50	$ 120.89		$ 107.40	$ 83.55	$ 82.86	
CCIE Online			$ 250.00		$ 600.00	$ 600.00	0	
CCIE Magazine			$ 150.00		$ 145.00	$ -	0	
Web: GoDaddy/Julie	$ 50.00	$ 50.00	$ 50.00		$ 50.00	$ -	$ -	
GotoWebinar fee							$ 400.00	
Direct mail						$ 430.00	0	
NCCA membership	$ 405.00					$ -	0	
Total Spend	$ 513.96	$ 144.50	$ 570.89	$ 1,229	$ 902.40	$1,113.55	$ 482.86	$ 2,498.81
Total # leads	62	94	102	258	130	119	193	442
Cost Per Lead	$ 8.29	$ 1.54	$ 5.60	$ 4.76	$ 6.94	$ 9.36	$ 2.50	$ 5.65
# New Customers	3	5	9	17	25	12	26	63
Conversion % Lead->Cust	5%	5%	9%	7%	19%	10%	13%	14%
Cost Per Customer	$ 171.32	$ 28.90	$ 63.43	$ 72.29	$ 36.10	$ 92.80	$ 18.57	$ 39.66
TOTAL REVENUE	$ 1,178	$ 2,835	$ 4,479	$ 8,492	$ 5,035	$ 3,325	$ 4,320	$ 12,680
Average Rev / Customer	$ 393	$ 567	$ 498	$ 500	$ 201	$ 277	$ 166	$ 201
Return on Investment/Cust.	229%	1962%	785%	691%	558%	299%	895%	507%

SOCIAL PROOF CHECKLIST

All the places you can and should have social proof, including testimonials, reviews, awards, and endorsements:

⇒ On your website

⇒ On your social media sites

⇒ On third party directories and search engines

⇒ Scrolling on a TV screen in your lobby (or a stationary iPad)

⇒ Framed on the walls of your business or in your lobby

⇒ Framed in the customer bathroom of your business

⇒ In your Company Newsletter that's mailed to customers

⇒ On your company vehicle

⇒ At the bottom of your email signature

⇒ In email blasts

⇒ In your brochures and marketing collateral

⇒ On your exterior signage / banners

⇒ On your hold music / answering machine message

⇒ On printed or digital ads

⇒ On hiring platforms like Indeed and Glassdoor

Remember, you can never have too much social proof!

Appendix

My Productivity and "Get Out of Overwhelm" Plan   Today's Date: _____

1. What 3 questions do I get asked most often by my employees, repeatedly?
   _____
   _____
   _____

2. How will I systematize the answers to these, to eliminate them from happening?
   _____
   _____
   _____

3. What time-wasting activities will I eliminate?
   _____
   _____
   _____

4. What "time vampires" will I manage and reduce?
   _____
   _____
   _____

5. How will I create more structure around my schedule and my time?
   _____
   _____
   _____

6. What new boundaries will I set?
   _____
   _____
   _____

7. What projects do I give myself permission to NOT take on?
   _____
   _____
   _____

THE ANTIDOTE TO FEAR

Kris Murray is an 8-figure entrepreneur who has built two companies from scratch and helped hundreds of business owners double or triple their businesses. She's an author of five books on business, leadership, and mindset as well as a professional speaker.

Kris now works with clients one on one and in small groups to help them find their ultimate freedom through strategic business coaching as well as transformational mindset coaching. She lives in the mountains of Colorado near Aspen, and has two grown children.

For more information on working with Kris, please visit **www.krismurray.com** or find her on Instagram at **@iamkrismurray**

MORE FROM THE AUTHOR - OTHER BOOKS BY KRIS MURRAY

The Ultimate Child Care Marketing Guide

77 Best Strategies to Grow Your Early Childhood Program

Rock Star Stories, Volume I

Rock Star Stories, Volume II

www.ingramcontent.com/pod-product-compliance
Lightning Source LLC
Chambersburg PA
CBHW071743120626
46550CB00002B/641